Liberty March
The Battle of Oriskany

Allan D. Foote
with James Morrison,
Joseph Robertaccio, and Alan Sterling

Illustrations by David Yahnke

LIBERTY MARCH
The Battle of Oriskany

Copyright © 1998
by
Allan D. Foote

ISBN 0-925168-72-6

Cover design: John Mahaffy

A joint publication

NORTH COUNTRY BOOKS, INC.
311 Turner Street
Utica, New York 13501
and
MOHAWK VALLEY HISTORY PROJECT
4 Cheriton Drive
Whitesboro, New York 13492

DEDICATION

*To my wife, Katherine, and my sons, Joshua, Jason, and Michael,
whose love and support made this body of work possible.*

*And in memory of Arthur A. Foote
30th Infantry Division, United States Army
A patriot and my father.*

CONTENTS

Acknowledgements...vii

Introduction...ix

Centennial...1

The Iroquois 17

The Loyalists.. 41

The Patriots 65

Revolution 91

The March 117

The Battle... 143

Aftermath 173

Appendix I: The Man Who Shot General Herkimer 193

Appendix II: Organization of the Tryon County Militia 197

Appendix III: Roster of the Tryon County Militia.................. 201

Endnotes 213

Bibliography 215

Index of Names 218

Photo by the author

Battle Creek, courtesy of New York State Office of Parks, Recreation
and Historic Preservation, Oriskany Battlefield State Historic Site

ACKNOWLEDGEMENTS

I am extremely grateful for the support and contribution made by so many individuals and organizations. They made possible the filtering of a significant body of information from the multitude of sources available. Without their generous and selfless assistance, my telling of the Oriskany saga could not have been accomplished. If I have mistakenly omitted anyone, I sincerely apologize.

My mother, Alice Bevington Foote; my in-laws, Hans and Jeanette Baumgartner; the outstanding research assistance of James Morrison, Joseph Robertaccio, and Alan Sterling; the illustrative talents of David Yahnke; Dot Hanrahan; the partners of the Harris Brothers Jewelers, Mena and Frank Carzo, Frank and Marianne Carzo for their encouragement and support.

Patricia Zemken; Brighid O'Brien, Bob Quist, the staff, and the Board of Trustees of the Utica Public Library; Patrick Huther and Bill Juteau of Kwik Copy; Nick Burns and Sheila Orlin of North Country Books; John Mahaffy; Audrey Sherman; Kevin Marken; Dick Williams; the Board of Directors and volunteers and staff of the Oneida County Historical Society.

Shirley Maring; Brian Patterson, Bear Clan representative of the Men's Council, the Oneida Indian Nation; volunteers and staff of the Shako:Wi Cultural Center; Joe Kelly, Oneida County Historian; and Kathy Kelly for her wise counsel; Joseph Caruso; Mike McHale of New Hartford True Value Hardware; Bill Lange, Park Ranger and the staff at the Fort Stanwix National Monument, National Park Service; the volunteers and staff of The Herkimer Home; Johnson Hall; Oriskany Battlefield; State of New York Historic Sites; Friends of Herkimer Home; Karen Jacobsen; volunteers of the Village of Oriskany Museum.

Donna Donovan and Mike Chalmers of the *Utica Observer Dispatch*; Steve Merren, Sam Weiss, and Mike Davis of WKTV; Scott Carr of WIBX radio; Jackie Phillips; Morris Sturdevant and the Friends of Oriskany Battlefield; Dr. John Johnsen and Dr. Frank Bergmann of Utica College of Syracuse University; Anthony Wayne Tommell, NYS Office of Parks, Recreation and Historic Preservation; New York Historical Society; staff and volunteers at Fort Johnson; Children's Museum of Utica; Dr. Evelyn Murphy; the Utica Symphony Orchestra; Montgomery County Historical

Society; Palatine Society; Fort Klock Historical Restoration; the staff of the Northern Frontier Project; Congressman Sherwood Boehlert; Senator Raymond Meier; Assemblyman David Townsend; Assemblywoman RoAnn Destito; County Executive Ralph Eannace; Village of Oriskany Mayor Donald Rothdiener.

David Drucker, Curator Shako:Wi Cultural Center; Gary Warshefski, Superintendent, Fort Stanwix National Monument; Nancy Demyttenaere, Regional Director, NYS Office of Parks, Recreation, and Historic Preservation; Mohawk Valley Heritage Corridor Commission; and Charles Schneider, Conductor Utica Symphony Orchestra.

And finally to the heroic American freedom fighters of all generations.

Allan D. Foote
Whitesboro, New York
August 6, 1998

What is history but a fable agreed upon?

—*Napoleon*

INTRODUCTION

Knifing through the rolling slopes of Oneida County in Upstate New York, near the place described by the Iroquois as the "Field of Nettles," is a precipitous ravine. At its base, a trickle of a brook lazily meanders through the wooded terrain. The simple tranquility of the site offers scant evidence to the visitor that over two centuries ago, this gentle stream was engorged with the blood of patriots.

At this unassuming location on the sixth of August 1777, seven hundred and sixty men of the patriot Tryon County Militia, allied with sixty Oneida Indian warriors, clashed with a mixed force of Iroquois and Loyalists in a pivotal engagement of the American War of Independence. The militia brigade and the Oneidas were marching to the relief of besieged Fort Stanwix when they were ambushed by Iroquois warriors (primarily Senecas and Mohawks), Tory rangers, and a detachment of the King's Royal Regiment of New York. As a result, the ground called Oriskany was forever sealed in the annals of United States history.

Drawing back the curtain of time, which transforms people, places, and events of the past into opaque shadows, can be an arduous task. Scrutinizing the circumstances pertaining to the action at Oriskany is no exception to this as truth has been supplanted by legend in some key elements of the story. This development has been exacerbated by the scarcity of primary sources, the self-serving reports of the major antagonists, the absence of any formal post-battle record by the militia commander, and the natural tendencies of old soldiers with fading memories to embellish their personal contributions to the glorious cause. Yet recent historical research has allowed us to paint a picture of that bloody day at Oriskany perhaps more complete than earlier studies of the battle. The "March" and "Battle" chapters will present a unique tactical analysis of the battle woven with the better known anecdotal descriptions from nineteenth century and early twentieth century writings.

In the early chapters the reader will find sketches of Mohawk Valley history prior to the Revolution detailing the experiences of three cultures which would clash in that wilderness inferno: Native American Iroquois,

Loyalist British, and Patriot Palatine. To appreciate these three groups' respective motivations in the American Revolution, it is necessary to have some basic understanding of the march of time which brought them on a collision course in the late eighteenth century in the valley of the Mohawk.

The people of the Mohawk Valley have, for the past two hundred years, kept the flame of tribute burning in their hearts and reflected in their deeds in remembrance of the struggle at Oriskany. These include writers, artists, poets, public officials and agencies, as well as private individuals and organizations. Yet in spite of their best efforts, the Oriskany saga is one which is glossed over or superficially treated by historians and authorities in the national arena.

The American people have largely forgotten the tremendous sacrifices made on this field of honor in defense of liberty. This is an injustice which should be rectified by restoration of the Battle of Oriskany to its rightful place of prominence in the military history of the United States. This can only be accomplished by further study and debate. The case for it is compelling:

- At Oriskany, the Tryon County Militia suffered a terrible casualty rate. This qualified the engagement as the bloodiest battle of the American War for Independence.
- At Oriskany, neighbor faced neighbor in the continent's first civil war.
- At Oriskany, America's first allies in war emerge; the Oneida Indian Nation.
- At Oriskany, because of the split in Iroquois loyalties, a three-hundred-year-old system of democratic governance known as "The Great Peace" comes to a cataclysmic end.
- Finally, there is the impact of Oriskany on the fortunes of war and the quest for liberty.

The smoke of battle had barely cleared on August 6, 1777, when apologists and revisionists began to warp the reality of what happened in that wilderness battle and its subsequent impact on the fate of a young nation.

There is no need to deify the men of the militia and their Oneida Indian allies for their stand on that battlefield, for this only serves to dehumanize their actions. The fact that one hundred fifty of their number held the field at three o'clock in the afternoon after a five-hour slugfest against a numerically superior enemy is glory enough. But they failed in their strategic mission to lift the siege of Fort Stanwix. However, the demoralization of the Crown's Indian allies, due to their losses at Oriskany, when coupled with Col. Peter Gansevoort's heroic defense of Fort Stanwix and Gen. Benedict Arnold's advance up the Mohawk Valley, did aid in the eventual withdrawal of British commander Barry St. Leger's troops.

Recent historical accounts have dispelled the myth that Sir William Howe was ordered to move north from New York City. Howe was never formally given instructions to rendezvous with John Burgoyne in Albany. A "junction of cooperation" was planned, not a physical uniting of their two armies. So we are left with how the failure of St. Leger's column to secure the valley impacted the eventual demise of "Gentleman Johnny" at Saratoga.

By 1777, the center of wheat production in the northeast had shifted to the fertile Hudson, Schoharie, and Mohawk Valleys. This area has been labeled as the "Breadbasket of the Revolution." The valleys were the primary supplier of foodstuffs for George Washington's main army. If St. Leger had been successful in seizing this strategically vital region, not only would Burgoyne's army have been fed for a year but the largest rebel force in North America would have been denied essential sustenance.

At Bennington, Freeman's Farm, and Bemis Heights the redcoats were defeated on the battlefield. With shrinking supply sources, Burgoyne's army now faced the prospect of starvation.

Taking all of this into consideration, it would be a fair statement to contend that the gallant stand of the Tryon County Militia and their Oneida Indian allies at Oriskany was the first blow struck in a series of events in the northern theater which were the turning point of the war; for they led to an alliance with France and decided the fate of a nation.

That which follows is the true story of a column of citizen soldiers who entered a ravine in upstate New York as Palatine settlers and Oneida Indians, and emerged as American heroes.

This generation can pay no better tribute to the pioneers
of the Mohawk Valley, than to rescue from oblivion
the true import of the deeds they did.
Utica Morning Herald and Daily Gazette, August 7, 1877

Chapter One

CENTENNIAL

Photo by the author

The Oriskany Battle Monument, courtesy of New York State
Office of Parks, Recreation, and Historic Preservation, Oriskany Battlefield State Historic Site

Utica, New York... Monday morning, August 6, 1877. It is today reported in the *Utica Morning Herald and Daily Gazette* that the remains of Lt. Col. George Armstrong Custer have arrived at Poughkeepsie. They will be held in a vault until October when the final funeral service will be performed.

Custer, the flamboyant leader of the Union cavalry, had captured the public's imagination in the recent American Civil War. His breastplate of fame had shone even brighter after having fought the Sioux and Cheyenne on the western plains. Custer, the vainglorious, who had led two hundred and ten troopers of his United States Seventh Cavalry Regiment to slaughter along the banks of the Little Big Horn River in southern Montana. The casualties were victims of Custer's presidential ambitions and tactical blundering as much as the Indians were.

But the bulk of the print in this day's edition of the *Utica Herald* was devoted to discussion of the upcoming centennial observance of another battle from America's past. And in this engagement, also, the temperament and pride of the American commander contributed to a military catastrophe. In this struggle Native Americans once again played a prominent role. After the last musket was discharged on that horrific day, a multitude of husbands, brothers, fathers, and sons lay stiff and cold in the gathering darkness. They had offered themselves as the ultimate sacrifice in the quest for liberty.

The story of this centennial commemoration began on the eighth of June 1877, at a special meeting of the Oneida Historical Society.* At this assembly, the following resolution was adopted:

"One hundred years from August 6, 1877, there occurred, near the junction of the Oriskany and Mohawk streams, the most desperate and sanguinary, and one of the most important battles of the American Revolution. On that spot the whole military force of the Mohawk Valley, preceding to the relief of besieged Fort Stanwix, encountered the invading army, and nearly one-half laid down their lives in defense of home and country. This conflict prevented the union of the invaders with Burgoyne, at the Hudson, and contributed to his surrender."[1] It was further resolved that a meeting be held on June 19, at the Common Council chambers in Utica, to make arrangements for the centennial celebration of the Battle of Oriskany, to take place on the battleground.

At a subsequent session, a thirty-six-member General Committee of Arrangements was appointed. Named as its chairman was a prominent citizen of Utica, John Seymour. He successfully nominated his more famous brother, Horatio Seymour, to deliver the welcoming address at the centennial gathering.

* Popularly known as Oneida County Historical Society since the 1980's.

One of Horatio's more well-known monikers was the "Sage of Deerfield." Seymour had been a two-time Democratic governor of New York State and was arguably the brightest star in the Mohawk Valley's political constellation. During his second gubernatorial term in 1863, he visited New York City at the time of the draft riots and made a conciliatory speech. This led publisher Horace Greeley to label him a "Copperhead," a term used to describe northerners who sympathized with the South. This unfair characterization was used against him when, in 1868, he was nominated as the Democratic candidate in the United States presidential election running against the great war hero Ulysses S. Grant. Grant won the election handily.

In 1876, Seymour was elected the first president of the Oneida Historical Society and hence, his central role one year later during the one hundred year anniversary of the Battle of Oriskany. But Seymour was only one of many political and civic leaders named to the committee.

The cities of Utica and Rome sent their respective mayors, Charles W. Hutchinson and James Stevens. Fulton County judge, McIntyre Fraser and Clinton judge, Othniel S. Williams, were members. Williams was an 1831 graduate and trustee of Hamilton College and became president of the Utica, Clinton, and Binghamton Railroad.

Selected as one of the speakers at the east stand on the battlefield during the exercises was the United States senator from Utica, Francis Kernan, the first Democrat from New York to hold this office in twenty-four years. In fact, in 1877 Oneida County had the unique distinction of having both Empire State United States Senate seats occupied by two of its citizens. The other was Roscoe Conkling, another Utican, who was conspicuous by his absence at the event. Though it is unknown what political infighting might have caused the famous senator to miss the celebration, he was represented by his proteges, Congressman William J. Bacon and State Assemblyman Samuel S. Lowery.

Another former ally of Conkling's in the group, who would give a keynote speech on August 6, was Ellis H. Roberts. Born in Utica in 1826, he attended Yale College and later served as principal of Utica Free Academy. He was known locally as editor and proprietor of the *Utica Morning Herald*, an avocation he embraced for forty-eight years, beginning in 1851. In both 1870 and 1872, he was elected to the U.S. Congress. He served under Presidents McKinley and Roosevelt as treasurer of the United States.

Two fascinating members of the Committee of Arrangements were Philo White and Joseph Porter. White was the grandson of early pioneer Hugh White, founder of Whitestown. Born in Whitestown in 1796, the restless young man moved to the Wisconsin territory where he was associated with newspapers and later embarked on a political career.

In 1853, Philo White was appointed by President Franklin Pierce as United States minister to the exotic South American country of Ecuador. He returned to his namesake hometown in 1858, and two years later donated a plot of land for the town courthouse and public green. He continued a proud family tradition of philanthropy and public service.

In 1856, as a boy of only ten years, Joseph Porter of Rome assisted his adoptive father in distributing anti-slavery literature among the farmers of Oneida County. An earnest abolitionist, he argued fervently on behalf of the slaves. At fourteen he made his first public speech in support of presidential candidate Abraham Lincoln. In September 1861, he became one of the first local enlistees in the Union army and received several wounds during the Battle of the Crater in Petersburg, Virginia in 1864.

Porter was the eternal optimist who "saw the good in everything." After the Civil War, he held the position of county clerk for twelve years. His contemporaries believed that old soldiers never had a better friend than Joseph Porter. With characteristic vigor, he succeeded in securing needed pensions for many Civil War veterans and widows.

Heading the Montgomery County delegation was the tycoon Commodore John Starin. During the "War Between the States," he had won the confidence of large military suppliers in New York City as a freight handler by expediting their shipments on the railways. After the end of hostilities, he turned his attention to harbor navigation and, at the peak of his career, his holdings included a total of 176 boats. His ornate brick mansion still stands in Fultonville.

Representing the host village of Oriskany was a member of one of the oldest families of the hamlet. George Graham's grandfather had come from Scotland in 1810 and started the first power loom in Oneida County. Mr. Graham was general manager of the Malleable Iron Company of Oriskany and held the distinction of having supervised the construction of exactly one mile of the Erie Canal.

A large number of the committee's complement included descendants of members of the patriot Tryon County Militia; the men who fought the Battle of Oriskany. Representatives of such well-known colonial Mohawk Valley families as Wagner, Visscher, Fonda, Bellinger, Fox, Timmerman, Roof, Walrath, Sammons, and Campbell were there.

Alfred J. Wagner of Fort Plain was unanimously chosen parade grand marshal. He was related to Lt. Col. Peter Wagner, second-in-command of the Second (Palatine District) Regiment of the Tryon County Militia. Fellow committeeman Webster Wagner of Palatine Bridge could also count Officer Wagner in his lineage. A prominent railroad manufacturer, Webster Wagner had, in 1859, invented the elevated sleeping car for the railroad by placing ventilators in the elevation. This was a major innovation for the time, significantly increasing the comfort level of passengers. In 1867, he achieved another success when he produced the first drawing room coach or palace car.

Maj. Douglass Campbell of Cherry Valley was the great-grandson of Lt. Col. Samuel Campbell, second-in-command of the First (Canajoharie District) Regiment; S.G. Visscher of Rome was descended from Col. Frederick Visscher, commander of the Third (Mohawk District) Regiment; and Peter F. Bellinger, who hailed from Herkimer County, was the grandson of Col. Peter Bellinger, commander of the Fourth (Kingsland & German Flatts District) Regiment, Tryon County Militia.

Noted authors and historians contributed to the battlefield commemoration on August 6 as committeemen and speakers. They included Daniel E. Wager of Rome, future scribe of *Our County and its People* (1896); Jeptha Simms, who in five years would release his two-volume treatise, *Frontiersmen of New York*; and county court judge Pomroy Jones of Lairdsville, who roamed the countryside gathering information for the region's first full-length history. He released *Annals and Recollections of Oneida County* in 1851.

The Battle of Oriskany Centennial Committee had men of military experience who were instrumental in the planning of the large parade march. One was Brig. Gen. Sylvester Dering of Utica, who had served in the New York State National Guard since his appointment by governor, and fellow Utican, Horatio Seymour in 1863.

Another was Oriskany's Maj. Alonzo King, who in civilian life was a dealer in cattle and hogs but who distinguished himself as a hero of the Civil War. He enlisted, in 1862, as a private in the 146th NY Infantry, and served in most of the major campaigns of the Army of the Potomac, including the Battle of the Wilderness. At the Battle of Five Forks, for refusing to leave the field after being wounded, he was promoted to major for gallant and conspicuous bravery. At the end of the war, in April of 1865, he was at Appomatox and witnessed Lee's surrender to Grant. On August 6, 1877, the Committee of General Arrangements for the Battle of Oriskany Centennial was fortunate to have a man of such high caliber as a member.

In the still of the early morning of August 6, Grand Marshal Alfred J. Wagner strapped on a sword decorated with a chased blade, the handle wound with gleaming gold wire. Wagner carried it in a scabbard made of worn leather adorned with silver clasps. One hundred years ago to the day his grandfather, Capt. Peter Wagner of the Second (Palatine District) Regiment of the Tryon County Militia, had wielded this same blade on the field of battle at Oriskany. The grand marshal proceeded to the headquarters of the General Committee of Arrangements situated at Bagg's Hotel in downtown Utica, one of the city's finest hotels. The establishment was under the proprietorship of fellow committee member, Thomas Redfield Proctor.

Proctor was emerging as a community philanthropist of stellar magnitude. In the latter part of the nineteenth century, he would gradually acquire and subsequently donate vast tracts of land to the people of Utica. The city's massive parks system and the Utica Public Library are a portion of this generous legacy.

Shortly after 7 A.M. on August 6, 1877, Alfred Wagner mounted his horse and began a pleasant ride to the place of rendezvous in the village of Oriskany. He was accompanied by Chief of Staff Everts and several aides. Along the route, couriers cantered ahead to ensure that the various parade divisions and detachments were in full readiness.

As the grand marshal made his way forward, he encountered a multitude of like-minded travelers embarked on the same pilgrimage. They came by the hundreds and thousands, from all directions...east, west, north, and south. The group journeyed by every mode of transportation imaginable. They glided along the waterways on steamers and packets, bumped along the dusty roads in carriages and wagons, and sped across the railways. And if no other option was available to them, they trusted in shoe leather.

As reported by the press, it was recognized that "...the quickest way to the battlefield is by rail; the coolest by boat; the most troublesome by vehicle."[2] But, regardless of the annoyance encountered, still they all came. Men, women, and children of every socio-economic class. On that day, all thoroughfares led to Oriskany.

No effort was spared to move the masses to the battlefield site. Though use of the Erie Canal was in the beginning stages of a long, slow descent into obsolescence, everything in the form of a scow, flat, packet tug, and steamer on the canal between Troy and Syracuse was requisitioned to carry passengers. The fare by steamer from Utica to and from the battlefield was fixed at twenty cents and round trip tickets were available at a reduced rate. A pontoon bridge was erected to aid patrons in reaching the railroad.

It is not surprising that the railroads had an important role to play on this day of the centennial observance of the Battle of Oriskany. The railroad companies were models of efficiency and service. The names of these grand enterprises from the golden era of the iron horse were: The Delaware, Lackawanna, and Western; Utica and Black River; Rome, Watertown & Ogdensburg; and of course, the New York Central.

Every available coach in Central New York was pressed into service and filled to capacity from the locomotive to the rear platform. All morning the trains ran from Syracuse, Schenectady, Binghamton, Watertown, and from seventy-two stops in between. From the New York Central's Tryon Station it was only a brief five-minute stroll to the battlefield. There were no mishaps, save for the Fulton and Montgomery County parade divisions bypassing their debarkation points and running on to the battlefield. A telegram was swiftly dispatched and the divisions were returned promptly to their rightful positions. The whole affair caused no more than a ten-minute delay in the proceedings. The entire operation was a testimony to superb organization on the part of railway officials and the General Committee of Arrangements.

At approximately 11:10 A.M., at the head of the massive column in the village of Oriskany, Alfred J. Wagner barked the command to advance to the battlefield, and the grand military and civic procession stirred slowly into motion.

It was the largest documented assemblage in the history of Oneida County. There were more than three thousand marchers organized by county, subdivided by township, and comprised of over 115 distinct groups. If stretched end to end, the column would have spanned over six miles in length.

The parade was led by members of the General Committee of Arrangements and by various political and civic leaders. Riding in a carriage with the Honorable Horatio Seymour, President of the Day, was special guest Mrs. Abraham Lansing of Albany, granddaughter of Col. Peter Gansevoort, who had been commander of the garrison at Fort Stanwix during the siege of 1777. Gently held in Mrs. Lansing's embrace was a flag from the American War of Independence. Shortly, the Gansevoort family would graciously share it once again with the people of the Mohawk Valley.

Governor Seymour and Mrs. Lansing were joined by Anne and Emily Greene and Adilda Eaton of Herkimer, New York and by Warren Herkimer of Jamesville, Wisconsin, descendants of Brig. Gen. Nicholas Herkimer, heroic commander of the Tryon County Militia. They carried with them a portrait of their courageous ancestor.

In all, over fifty descendants of members of the Tryon County Militia are known to have been in attendance. They were identified by a red, white, and blue badge worn over their left breasts. Every principal militia brigade officer was represented except Col. Ebenezer Cox, who had led the First Regiment (Canajoharie District) into the bloody ravine at Oriskany a century before. The absence of any representation for the unfortunate Colonel Cox may be the result of his influence over General Herkimer just before the battle.

At the head of the Montgomery and Fulton Counties contingent was Commodore Starin. Riding with him was Chester A. Arthur, the forty-seven-year-old collector of the port of New York, who served as his chief of staff. Since 1863, this debonair gentleman had been a member of Roscoe Conkling's New York Republican political organization. The collector post was perhaps the most powerful and profitable patronage job in the nation as it involved handling two-thirds of all U.S. tariff revenues.

Arthur, recognized as a skilled mediator and dedicated public servant, would be nominated vice president of the United States and, in 1881, following the assassination of James Garfield, would become our twenty-first president. Though his presidency was plagued by party fragmentation and mediocre legislative achievements, on August 6, 1877, Chester Alan Arthur's political future glistened before him as he rode to Oriskany.

Behind the Montgomery and Fulton groups came Herkimer and Oneida Counties' participants. There were seventeen military groups representing the army, national guard, and the minutemen's organizations popular during this era; four artillery batteries; eighteen police and fire units; two steamer companies; sixteen military and civilian musical groups dominated by drum corps and cornet bands. The city of Rome's division contained a single resolute company personifying America's first allies in war, the Oneida Indian Nation.

Each county had its contingent of grizzled veterans from the United States' second and last conflict with England, the War of 1812. Most of the men were now well into their eighties, and they were reverentially given seats of honor in horse-drawn carriages. It was noted that as the years rolled by, the number of old soldiers was dwindling significantly. At the time of the centennial, less than sixty stalwart survivors remained in all of Oneida County.

In contrast, a dozen other units of veterans marched on foot with the vigor expected of men in the prime of their lives. They had won glory and saved the Union as soldiers of the Grand Army of the Republic just twelve years before. Their names were "forever emblazoned on fame's immortal scrolls." To honor the defenders of liberty at Oriskany, they once again donned the faded blue uniforms of their youth, proudly lifted their battle flags high, and smartly stepped down another dusty road.

They included the men of the 97th New York, known as "Conkling Rifles," formed primarily of boys from Herkimer and Oneida Counties. As part of "Fighting Joe" Hooker's 1st Corps at Antietam, the 97th had smashed into Stonewall Jackson's rebel troops in a cornfield and sent them reeling.

At Gettysburg, the regiment was called on to help plug the gap in the Union salient on Seminary Ridge on the first day. They suffered horrific losses, but helped buy the Army of the Potomac valuable time to build up reinforcements and defensive positions on the high ground of Cemetery Hill by evening.

The first sons of the Mohawk Valley to heed their nation's call in 1861 had been the men of the 14th N.Y. Infantry. As part of Hunter's Division at First Bull Run, the regiment had been part of the sweeping flank which surprised the southern left position. Today, their numbers were amply represented in the grand procession.

Also tramping to Oriskany on this hot and dusty morning were veterans of the 146th New York (also known as the 5th Oneida). On the second day of the Battle of Gettysburg, they were brigaded under the command of Gen. Stephen Weed. As John Bell Hood's Texans clambered up the steep slopes of famed Little Round Top, Weed's brigade ably defended the northern portion of the hill.

Undoubtedly, former soldiers of the 26th, 34th, 117th, and 121st New York Infantry Regiments were also sprinkled throughout the contingents of various Grand Army of the Republic posts. In all, it is estimated that up to twenty-five thousand men and women of the Mohawk Valley served in the army, navy, and medical corps of the United States during the War of the Rebellion. You will find the final resting place of those who "gave the last full measure of their devotion" in many of the tranquil cemeteries which dot the valley today.

As the lengthy entourage snaked its way the few short miles from the village to the battlefield, they were treated to a festive reception by the populace along the route. Evergreens, flags, colorful banners, Chinese lanterns, and flowers festooned from private homes and public buildings. The route which General Herkimer and his troops had taken in 1777 was marked by neatly painted signs. One enterprising and sentimental woman had braided the words "Gen Herkimer" in ferns on a white background. It was accented by a wreath with the year "1777" crafted on it and an evergreen arch over the roadway.

Martial music filled the air as the many melodic ensembles competed for the public's ear. Some of these bands of local renown included Sherman's Band of New Hartford, the 26th Battalion Band, Herkimer's Old Brass Band, and the Old Utica Band. There were cornet bands from Johnstown, Mohawk, Clinton, Oriskany, and Rome. The staccato pounding of the numerous drum corps echoed the sound of the marcher's footsteps. Along the road and at the battlefield, cannon added their booming bass voices in salute.

As the grand military and civic procession approached the battlefield, they encountered an awesome spectacle. The main road, the by-ways, hills, valleys, and surrounding farmlands were dark with people as far as the eye could see. There was seemingly no end to this sea of humanity begrimed with dust. Conservative calculations estimated the crowd at over sixty thousand people.

The incredible scene was well-documented by the national media, underlining the importance of the engagement at Oriskany in American history. Journalists in attendance represented such newspapers as the *New York Herald*, *Albany Journal*, *Syracuse Courier*, *Rome Sentinel*, *Pittsburgh Telegraph*, and *Chicago Times*. Many of the descriptions of the day's activities provided here are due to the excellent reporting of the correspondents of the *Utica Morning Herald and Daily Gazette*.

As the head of the column entered the battlefield, the various military formations lining both sides of the road presented arms and fired off salutes. The crowds behind them pressed forward and cheered enthusiastically. Suddenly, General Dering came dashing over a hill with the Rome Cavalry Troop close on his heels. Surrounding the natural amphitheater of the sacred ground, the military units were positioned on the slopes. They included the 21st Brigade, Utica Citizen's Corps, Adjutant Bacon Cadets, and 26th Battalion. The elevation gave them a magnificent panoramic view of the lush green hills of the Mohawk Valley.

At approximately 12:20 P.M. on August 6, 1877, one hour and ten minutes after departing the village of Oriskany, Governor Seymour led the procession past the ravine where so many of General Herkimer's gallant militiamen had fallen one hundred years before. The troops honored the spot by bringing their arms to the carry position and solemnly dipping their colors. Meanwhile, the enormous audience continued to signify their approval with unrestrained hurrahs.

The point of the column rolled to the west of the battlefield, then pivoted to the north along the line of the grand marshal's field headquarters, then shifted to the east past the main grandstand where Governor Seymour and Mrs. Lansing alighted with other orators and guests. The procession continued to wheel around the grounds until a hollow square was formed around the principal body of spectators and the grandstand. Finally, the massive military and civic formation came to a rest.

As the crowd settled to a low murmur, Rev. Dr. Edward Martin Van Deusen, rector of Grace Church in downtown Utica, was called upon to offer a prayer. As the audience bowed their heads, Reverend Van Deusen began, "O God, who art the blessed and only Potentate, the King of Kings and Lord of Lords; the Almighty ruler of nations; we adore and magnify thy glorious name for all the great things which thou hast done for us. We especially desire on this hundredth anniversary of a great struggle and victory, to acknowledge thy over-ruling Providence in all things, and raise a memorial of thy living kingdom and tell out thy works with gladness. We render thee thanks for the goodly heritage which thou hast given us; for the civil and religious privileges which we enjoy; and for the multiplied manifestations of thy favor toward us."[3]

At the conclusion of Dr. Van Deusen's invocation, George Graham of Oriskany introduced the honorable Horatio Seymour, who delivered the welcoming address. The governor calmly rose to polite applause and proceeded to begin perhaps the finest speech of his celebrated career.

Seymour commenced, "All who care for the glory of our country; all who love to study the history of events which have shaped our civilization, government and laws; all who seek to lift up the virtues of our people by filling their minds with lofty standards of patriotism, will rejoice that we meet here today on this battlefield to honor the courage and devotion displayed here one hundred years ago. The men of the valley of the Mohawk will be wiser and better for this gathering upon the spot where their fathers fought and suffered and bled to uphold the cause of this country."

The governor touched further upon the profound misery that had been heaped upon the people of the region during the Revolution and how it should be commemorated. "The old churches and homes built when Britain ruled our country, and which were marred by war when this valley was desolated by torch and tomahawk, will grow more sacred in our eyes. Their time-worn walls will teach us in their silent way to think of the suffering, of bloodshed, more dreadful and prolonged than were endured elsewhere during the revolutionary struggle. Let us who live along the course of the Mohawk now enter upon our duty of making its history as familiar as household words. Let us see that the graves of dead patriots are marked by monuments."

Seymour spoke of the valley's historic role in the ongoing development of the nation. "At our feet are railroads and water routes that have been for a series of years the thoroughfares for a vast current of commerce, and the greatest movement of the human race recorded in its history. All other movements, in war or peace, are insignificant in comparison with the vast numbers that have passed along the borders of this battlefield to find homes in the great plains of the West, to organize social systems and to build up great states. The currents of events which distinguish our history, like the currents of our rivers, have largely had their origin in our territory."[4]

The attentive and appreciative audience interrupted the governor's speech regularly with enthusiastic applause. Seymour continued, "It is a source of patriotic pride to those who live in this valley that the flag of our country, with the stars and stripes, was first displayed in the face of our enemies on the banks of the Mohawk by the defenders at Fort Stanwix. Here it was baptized in the blood of battle. Here it first waved in triumph over a retreating foe." (The reader should note that many historians dispute this claim. News of the emblem adopted by the Continental Congress for the standards to be borne by its troops did not reach Albany until early August 1777, too late for the information to have reached the fort then under siege. Subsequent testimony by defenders of the wilderness garrison indicates that a handmade battle flag was sewn from strips of red, white, and blue cloth into stripes; however there is no mention of any stars).

Seymour went on, "Time has destroyed that standard. But I hold in my hand another banner hardly less sacred in its association with our history. It is the flag of our state which was borne by the regiment commanded by Colonel Gansevoort, not only here at the beginning of the Revolutionary War, but also when it was ended by the surrender of the British army at Yorktown."⁵

This was the flag which Gansevoort's granddaughter, Mrs. Abraham Lansing, had carefully brought with her from Albany. The sacred relic consisted of a piece of heavy, fine quality silk of a vibrant blue color. It was square-shaped and seven feet in size and marked with fringe. Painted in the center was an oval shield upon which was depicted the sun rising from behind a mountain peak, the foot of which reached down to the water. Above the shield was an eagle standing upon a hemisphere. The shield was supported on either side by female figures about two feet high; on the left was "Liberty"; on the right, "Justice," holding the even balance; and at the bottom was a scroll bearing the word "Excelsior." The design upon the flag was a precursor to the seal of the State of New York adopted in 1778.

This national treasure showed the ravages of time. The paint was cracked and the silk shredded throughout. Still, it had been passed down to posterity to be treated with reverence and affection. Colonel Gansevoort had handed it to his descendants in trust and Mrs. Lansing had taken loving care of it. She obligingly made the trip west to share it with the multitude at Oriskany.

Seymour thanked Mrs. Lansing for her kind favor as his brother John lifted the banner aloft. It floated proudly in the breeze. The vast congregation gave three boisterous cheers, throwing their hats into the air. The military units presented arms and the massed bands played the "Star Spangled Banner." An artillery battery accented the moment with a roaring salute. The ambiance was electrifying.

Earlier in his speech, Governor Seymour had spoken of early legends of the valley of the Mohawk; of a great nation which ruled the region without battle flags. They were masters of the mountains, rivers, and valleys for over one hundred years until the coming of the Europeans. They were the Iroquois.

Horatio Seymour, from Wager's *Our
County and its People,* collection of
the Oneida County Historical Society

Daniel Wager, from Wager's, *Our
County and its People,* collection of the
Oneida County Historical Society

Philo White, from Durant's *History of
Oneida County,* collection of the
Oneida County Historical Society

Alonzo King, from Brainard's *Campaigns of the 146th* Regiment, collection of the Utica Public Library

In the valley of the Mohawk, from Greene's *The Mohawk Valley*

The Western Ravine at the Oriskany Battlefield in 1848, from Lossing's *Pictorial Field Book of the American Revolution*, collection of the Oneida County Historical Society

There is no such word as *wild* in the Indian languages.
The closest we can get to it is the word *free*. We were free people.
—Oren R. Lyons
Chief of the Turtle Clan, Onondaga Nation

Chapter Two

THE IROQUOIS

Statue of Red Jacket, Forest Lawn Cemetery, Buffalo,
New York

PEACEMAKER

The following discourse on the founding of the Confederacy of the Five Nations is based on the oral tradition of the Iroquois as recorded by Arthur C. Parker in 1916. In this story both historical and mythical elements are mixed, but more important it is the traditional saga accepted by the Iroquois people as it pertains to their roots as a unified league.

In the late fifteenth century a child was born in the land of the Crooked Tongues in the Huron village of Kahanahyenh by a long, winding bay north of the lake called Ontario.

Legend tells us that the infant was conceived of a virgin maiden. Just prior to the birth, the young girl slipped into a long, deep slumber and dreamed that her child would be a son whom she should name "Peacemaker." The messenger in the dream told her that her son would become a great man, that he would go among the people of the Flint (Mohawks) and that he would also travel to the Many Hill Nation (Onondagas) and there raise up the Great Tree of Peace.

As foretold, the virgin maiden gave birth to a son. The child's superstitious grandmother was distressed and rebuked her daughter. "You refuse to tell me the father of the child," she said, "and now how do you know a great calamity will not befall us, and our nation? You must drown the child."[1]

The dutiful daughter took her baby boy to the bay where she customarily drew water, chopped a hole in the ice, and thrust him in, but when night came the child was found at his mother's bosom. The next day the mother again took the child and flung him into the icy water, but at night he once again reappeared. The third time the grandmother herself took the boy and drowned him, but in the morning he was found, as before, nestled against his mother's bosom.

The grandmother marveled and exclaimed, "Mother, now nurse your child for he may become an important man."[2] From that moment on, the mother took gentle care of her infant and named him Peacemaker in accordance with the instructions of the spiritual messenger in her dream.

The child grew into young manhood remarkably strong and healthy, and was strikingly handsome in appearance. He was extremely honest and always candid in expressing his views, yet his fellow tribesmen scorned him, for he hated war. His lyrical voice soared against war around the campfires when battle was being planned. The Hurons' hearts grew bitter toward this peculiar man who "loved not war better than all things."[3] There was no place for this misfit in the land of the Crooked Tongues and jealous warriors conspired to drive him away.

Leaving his homeland behind, Peacemaker journeyed by canoe across the great lake of Ontario and came into the hunting territory of the people of the Flint. He made his way gradually south through the colossal forests until he came to "the great falls of the Mohawk." There in the swirling mist of the cascading waters, he told the people of the Flint that "The Great Creator from whom we all are descended sent me to establish the "Great Peace" among you. No longer shall you kill one another and nations shall cease warring upon each other. Such things are entirely evil and He, your Maker, forbids it. Peace and comfort are better than war and misery for a nation's welfare."

Still there were doubters among the Mohawks. To demonstrate his power as the messenger of the Creator, Peacemaker told the skeptics this, "By the side of the falls near the edge of a precipice stands a tall tree. I will climb the tree and seat myself in the topmost branches. Then you shall cut down the tree and I will fall into the depths below. Will that not destroy me?"[4]

The divine leader ascended the tree and it was chopped down. A multitude of spectators saw him hurtled into the chasm and plunged into the water. Evening came but Peacemaker did not appear and the people were satisfied he had perished.

Dawn came and the warriors saw strange fumes arising from the smoke hole of a vacant cabin. Cautiously they approached and peered through loose bark on the outside wall of the dwelling. To their amazement, there crouched Peacemaker preparing his morning meal.

The witnesses reported the revelation to the tribal chieftains and general population, and all were convinced that this messiah might indeed establish the Great Peace.

HAYONWATHA

Meanwhile, in the land of the Many Hills resided a man overcome with tremendous grief and bitterness. One by one all seven of his daughters had died. Nothing could console him in his immense sorrow. He declared, "I shall cast myself away, I shall bury myself in the forest, I shall become a woodland wanderer." And so he departed from the nation of the Onondaga, heading south. He was called Hayonwatha.

It is said that when he began his exodus, the heavens split and the skies were rent asunder.

That first night Hayonwatha slept on a mountain. On the second day he descended and camped at the base of the lofty peak. On the third day he journeyed onward and when evening came he camped in a hickory grove. It was on the next morning that he came to a place where round-jointed rushes grew. He paused as he saw them and made three strings from them and when he had built a fire he said: "This I would do if I found anyone burdened with grief even as I am. I would console them for they would be covered with night and wrapped in darkness. This would I lift with words of condolence and these strands of beads would become words with which I would address them."[5]

When daylight came he wandered on again and, altering the course of his journey, he turned to the east. At night he came to a group of small lakes, and upon one he saw a flock of ducks. There were so many swimming so closely together that they looked like a raft.

"If I am truly noble," he said to himself, "I shall here discover my power." He then spoke and said, "Oh you who are 'floats' lift up the water and permit me to pass over the bottom of the lake dryshod."

In a compact body the ducks suddenly flew upward, lifting the water of the lake with them. Thus did Hayonwatha walk down to the shore and upon the surface of the lake. There he noticed, in layers, the empty shells of the water snail, some white and others purple. Stooping down he filled a pouch of deerskin with the shells and then passed on to the other shore. Then the ducks swiftly descended and replaced the water of the lake. Evening came and he feasted on three roasted ducks. Thus the fifth day of his journey ended.

In the morning he ate the cold meat of the ducks and resumed his journey eastward. He spent the day hunting small game and resting. At dawn on the seventh day he nourished himself and turned once again to the south. Late in the evening he came to a clearing and found a bark hut. Once again he found shelter. He erected two poles, placed a third across the top and suspended three shell strings. Viewing them he said: "Men boast of what they would do in extremity but they do not do what they say. If I should see anyone in deep grief, I would remove these shell strings from the pole and console them. The strings would become words and lift away the darkness with which they are covered."

The next morning a small girl spotted smoke rising from the lodge; she crept up to it and listened. Then she sneaked forward and peered through a chink in the bark. Then, in haste, she ran home and told her father of the strange man she had seen. "The stranger must be Hayonwatha," said the father. "I have heard that he has departed from Onondaga. Return, my daughter, and invite him to our house." The young child obeyed and soon Hayonwatha accompanied her to the house. "We are about to hold a council," the father said. "Sit in that place on one side of the fire and I will acquaint you with our decisions."

The council of five chiefs was convened, and for two days there was great discussion. Before darkness every evening the council dissolved, and at no time was Hayonwatha called upon for advice nor was anything officially reported to him.

On the tenth day of his journey, as the debate continued in the council, the worthless guest, Hayonwatha, quietly left and resumed his wandering. Late in the evening he came to the perimeter of another settlement and as had become his custom he kindled a fire and erected a horizontal pole on two upright poles. Once again he placed the three strings of wampum shells and repeated his vow of condolence.

The head man of the village saw the smoke at the edge of the forest and sent a messenger to discover who the stranger might be. As the messenger approached the man seated before the fire, he heard the sentiments being spoken and observed the wampum shells. Without a word he left and returned to report what he had witnessed.

The head man responded. "The person whom you describe must truly be Hayonwatha. He it is who shall meet the great man foretold by the dreamer. We have heard that this man should work with the prophet who talks of the establishment of peace." The messenger returned to Hayonwatha with greetings and served as his escort back to the village.

Once again Hayonwatha sat as a mute guest at another lengthy council debate. For seven days he tolerated their indecision. No report was made to him, and so he was not even aware of the topics being discussed.

On the eighteenth night of his journey a runner came from the south. He told the chiefs of the eminent man residing in the village of the Mohawk River at the lower falls. The messenger said : "We know of the great man who came from the north. Now another great man will go forward in haste to meet him in the land of the Flint people. There shall the two councils meet and establish the Great Peace."

PEACEMAKER AND HAYONWATHA MEET

On the twenty-third day of his journey, Hayonwatha was brought to the home of Peacemaker. As Hayonwatha entered the hut, Peacemaker arose and spoke: "My younger brother, I perceive that you have suffered from some deep grief. You are a chief among your people and yet you are wandering about."

Hayonwatha answered, "My family of seven daughters has been destroyed. My sorrow and rage has been bitter." Peacemaker invited Hayonwatha to dwell with him and offered to represent his sorrow to the people of the village.

The council of the village deliberated but could reach no conclusion to remedy Hayonwatha's troubles. Peacemaker heard Hayonwatha say in frustration, "It is useless, for the people only boast what they will do, but they do nothing at all. If what had befallen me should happen to them, I would take down the three shell strings from the upright pole and I would address them and I would console them."

Peacemaker came forward and said to Hayonwatha, "My younger brother, it has now become very plain to my eyes that your sorrow must be removed. Your grief and rage has been great. I shall now undertake to remove your sorrows so that your mind may be rested."[6]

And Peacemaker took shells from Hayonwatha's deerskin pouch and strung a number of wampum beads. As he addressed Hayonwatha, Peacemaker handed him the strings of beads. Hayonwatha's mind and heart were soothed by Peacemaker's sympathetic words.

THE FORMATION OF THE CONFEDERACY

Peacemaker concluded, "My junior brother, your mind being cleared, we now shall make our laws and when all are made we shall call the organization we have formed the Great Peace. It shall be the power to abolish war and robbery between brothers and bring peace and tranquility."

And when they had finished this arduous task, Peacemaker said: "My younger brother, we shall now propose to the Mohawk Council the plan we have made. We shall tell them of our plan for a confederation and the building of a longhouse of peace. It will be necessary to have their consent to proceed." Peacemaker spoke to the council about establishing this union of all nations. The Mohawk enthusiastically agreed. Next, messengers were sent to their neighbors to the west, the people of the Stone (Oneida). Their chief, Odatshedeh, asked for a day to consider. The next day the answer came from the Oneida Council, "We will join the confederation."

Over the next five years, messengers scurried back and forth over the two hundred and fifty mile region of the Iroquois people—to the Onondaga of the central area; their neighbors to the west, the Cayuga; and the Seneca on the western flank. Peacemaker and Hayonwatha were tireless in their quest to establish the Great Peace. One by one, councils of the tribes agreed. Finally, representatives of all the five nations assembled in the land of the Onondaga. Peacemaker concluded, "Now indeed we may establish the Great Peace. I am Peacemaker and with the Five Nations' Confederate Lords I plant the Tree of the Great Peace... I name the tree the 'Tree of the Great Long Leaves.' "

A SYSTEM OF GOVERNANCE

At a time when most of Europe was ruled by iron-fisted, autocratic, imperial authority, Peacemaker presented to the people of the Five Nations a system of governance known as Gayanashagowa or The Great Binding Law. Some historians claim that this highly democratic political system of the Iroquois League may have served as a model for the authors of the United States Constitution.

The Great Binding Law was based upon already existing family, clan, and community organizations. Its aim was not only to unite its members through symbolic kinship relationships but to maintain the autonomy of individual tribal members. The league's Grand Council consisted of fifty male sachems appointed for life.

These peace chiefs were nominated by the clan mother of each sachem-producing lineage in each clan. The Onondaga had fourteen sachems, the Cayuga ten, the Oneida and Mohawk nine each, and the Seneca eight. This unequal tribal representation was compensated for by major decisions having to be reached through unanimity.

Gayanashagowa is divided into fourteen sections covering the following subjects touching upon all aspects of the Iroquois way of life. They are defined as: Rights, duties, and qualifications of Lords; Names, duties, and rights of war chiefs; Clans and consanguinity; Official symbolism; Laws of adoption; Laws of emigration; Rights of foreign nations; Rights and powers of war; Treason or secession of a nation; Rights of the people of the Five Nations; Religious ceremonies protected; The installation song; Protection of the longhouse; and Funeral addresses.

Each of the Five Nations had their distinct role in the governance of the Confederacy. The Iroquois envisioned their union symbolically as a great longhouse stretching from the land of the Mohawk near present day Albany to the Great Lakes to the west in the land of the Seneca. The Mohawk were "keepers of the eastern door." The Onondaga were "keepers of the fire," who kept the wampum of the league and consequently preserved the archives and served as the unofficial capital of the confederacy. The Seneca were guardians of the strategic "western door" and were particularly feared and respected as warriors. The Oneida and Cayuga people constituted the "younger" or junior members of the league.

The Grand Council held confederacy meetings at least once a year, but would congregate whenever an important issue needed to be discussed. In general the council would deal with intertribal matters, trade negotiations with foreigners, and deliberations of war and peace. There were originally fifty confederacy chiefs, but eventually two of these titles were left unfilled to honor the league's founders, Peacemaker and Hayonwhatha.

The Five Nations were divided into two parts mirroring the kinship division of the clans. The Elder moiety consisted of the Mohawk, Onondaga, and Seneca: the Oneida and Cayuga constituted the Younger. Seating at Grand Council meetings was arranged by nation and moiety. The Mohawk and Seneca sat on one side, the Oneida and Cayuga sat on the other, the Onondaga were in the middle position in front of the council fire.

As previously mentioned, all decisions of the council had to be unanimous. Deliberations began according to a set sequence of events. The topic under discussion was announced by the Onondaga, who then handed it to the Mohawk for consideration. When they concluded it was passed to the Seneca chiefs. After their deliberation, it was passed back to the Mohawk who announced their joint decision. The matter was then passed over the council fire to the Oneida and Cayuga, who exchanged discussion between themselves. After the Oneida declared their decisions to the Mohawk, a Mohawk chief declared the outcome to the Onondaga. If the Onondaga agreed as well, the decision was unanimous and a final ceremonial declaration was made by an Onondaga chief. At the conclusion of the ceremony, the final actions of the council were "read into" belts of wampum which recorded significant events of historical importance to the Iroquois.

If consensus was not achieved, the issue was given back to the Mohawk for further deliberation, beginning the process of negotiation over again. If a unanimous decision seemed impossible to reach, the matter was set aside. In a ritual act, the council fire was covered up with ashes. To the Iroquois it was important that all should be of "one heart, one mind, one law."

In addition, war chiefs and clan mothers could appoint a representative to have their opinions heard at council meetings. This complex democratic structure achieved remarkable results over three centuries. It would take the American Revolution to tear it asunder.

The complex union of governance developed by the Five Nations is admired by historians for its sophistication. It was achieved in part because the Mohawk, Oneida, Onondaga, Cayuga, and Seneca tribes shared closely related languages, similar cultural traits, and a need for cooperative defensive measures in time of conflict.

DOMESTIC LIFE

The Iroquois lived in large longhouses made of forked wooden poles fastened into the ground and covered with earth and bark. The most common types of bark used included cedar, elm, ash, fir, and spruce. Crossed poles were secured to the forked tops of the uprights so as to form an arched roof. Large sheets of bark were then tied onto the frame, rough side out. Rafters were affixed to the roof frame. These dwellings generally measured about twenty-five feet in width and eighty feet in length. At set intervals there were smoke holes in the roof. These would be covered by a moveable piece of bark when not in use. The hearth below each smoke hole would be shared by two families.

At each end of the longhouse there was a door of either animal hide or bark. Bunks along the inside wall served as beds at night and seating during the day. An overhead shelf was used for storage of food and utensils, strands of corn, dried fish, and other foods hung from poles overhead. Large bins made of bark were placed between each family's quarters within the longhouse. These bins were used to store corn, dried fruit, and cured meat. At the ends of the lodges firewood was stacked for cooking and heating. The front door of the house would often be adorned with carved or painted symbols of the clan residing within. Each longhouse would usually contain several families of the same matrilineage.

The longhouses would be clustered in stockaded villages located in easily defensible terrain and near a supply of drinking water. Close proximity to lakes and rivers was preferred as these provided the major routes of travel. A small hamlet may only have had a half-dozen structures, while a large village may have contained over one hundred lodges.

The roles of men and women were clearly defined in Iroquoia. Agriculture was a woman's enterprise. The females of the clan planted seed in the spring, weeded fields throughout the summer, and harvested crops in the fall. They would grow many varieties of corn, beans, and squash, commonly known as the "Three Sisters."[7] Sunflowers were raised for their oil which was used for cooking and hair dressing. Tobacco was grown and cherished for use in religious rituals. Because women performed all the farm work, they were considered owners of the family crops and fields. They controlled the distribution of all the food in their household. Particularly powerful women would dictate what land could be used by each member of the family.

Women and girls would also gather wild berries, fruits, nuts, and other edible woodland products. Sassafras roots, birch bark, spicewood, and hemlock twigs were boiled in hot water for use as beverages. Maple sugar or syrup were used as sweeteners.

The men provided sustenance for their families by fishing and by hunting wild fowl and animals. They procured deer, elk, moose, bear, beaver, partridge, and wild turkey. Bows and arrows were the basic hunting equipment, although wooden traps were sometimes utilized for larger game and spears and nets were used to catch fish and waterfowl. Women would often accompany the men on the major hunting expeditions to attend to camp needs. Sometimes men and women would organize communal deer hunts with over one hundred animals as the prize.

Women made clothing from animal hides, and in cold weather would cover themselves with extra pelts. Footwear mostly consisted of moccasins.

Iroquois families were related on the basis of descent through their women. This kinship system linked generations from mother to daughter. The society was divided into groups of people, or clans, and they considered themselves related and were usually named after animals, such as the bear, wolf, or turtle. They believed they had a spiritual connection to these animals.

Marriage in the Five Nations was celebrated with simplicity. Accompanied by her mother and some female relatives, the bride-to-be traveled to the house of her intended groom. When she arrived, she gave a present of corn bread to her future mother-in-law, who returned the honor with a token of deer meat. Those in attendance then enjoyed a feast. The exchange of these foods was symbolic, as corn represented the labor of women and deer meat the labor of men. Together these foods signified the interdependence of husband and wife in the economic well-being of the family.

In their leisure time the Iroquois enjoyed a variety of games, often coupled with betting on individual contestants or teams. One popular sport involved a small deerskin ball being carried through one of two gates erected on either side of a playing field. Two teams of participants handling long sticks with a small net at one end attempted to block their opponents and intercept the ball. This ancient tribal game was the precursor to the modern version of lacrosse.

BELIEFS AND CUSTOMS

The Iroquois recognized the existence of two major spiritual forces in the universe, called the "Twin Boys." The good twin was "Creator" or "Upholder of the Sky," and was responsible for all positive things on earth; the nourishing plants, rivers, useful animals, and man. The evil twin, "Flint" or "Evil-Minded One," had created the poisonous plants, vicious animals, and catastrophic events. There were also several lesser good and bad spirits who served the Creator and Evil-Minded One.

The people of the Five Nations kept a ritual calendar of festivals which primarily centered around their agricultural cycle. From the sweet nectar of the maple in the spring to the fall harvest of plenty, the Iroquois conducted observances of thanksgiving to express gratitude to the Creator for the bountiful gifts he showered upon them.

In Iroquois tradition, the fulfillment of one's night dreams was also considered necessary to prosper and maintain health and success. To the people of the Five Nations, their dreams were expressions of their innermost thoughts and desires. All community members were obliged to help a dreamer achieve his or her wish. This system of mutual aid served to bind the community together.

The use of strings or belts of wampum had great ritual value to the Iroquois. Wampum was generally made from clam shells obtained in trade with Indians from Long Island and the New Jersey shore. The shells were cut into pieces and made into small beads. These beads were strung together or woven into belts. Different patterns formed by the white and purple beads conveyed different messages.

Wampum was used to commemorate significant events such as visits by esteemed guests, funerals, or the signing of treaties with other nations. An account of the important event was "talked into the wampum" and thereby preserved for posterity.

Within the secure confines of their regional boundaries, the Iroquois of the early sixteenth century led what seemed, outside of an occasional border skirmish with their neighboring rivals, the Algonquins and Hurons, an idyllic existence. Warfare was less about empire building and more about defense and displaying acts of courage on the part of warriors. As prescribed by the Great Binding Law, captives were sometimes adopted into the tribal families.

An early Dutch visitor to the Mohawk territory described the environment as such:

"The land is good and fruitful in everything... The country is very mountainous and thereon grow the finest fir trees... In the forests, and here and there along the water side, there grows an abundance of chestnuts, plums, hazel nuts, large walnuts of several sorts. The ground on the hills is covered with bushes of blueberries; the ground in the flat land is covered with strawberries, which grow here so plentifully in the fields, that one can lie down to eat them... I have seen whole pieces of land where grapevine stood by grapevine and grew very luxuriantly, climbing to the top of the loftiest trees. In the forests is great plenty of deer and partridges, pigeons and hens which fly together in thousands, and a great number of all kinds of fowl, swans, geese, ducks which sport upon the river in thousands. Besides the deer and elks, there are panthers, bears, wolves, and foxes. In the river is a great plenty of all kinds of fish—pike, eels, perch, cat fish, sun fish, bass, and sturgeon."[8]

Through their belief in the Creator and the planting of the Tree of the Great Peace, the Iroquois people had achieved a strong communal bond with nature and their fellow man. The European quest for territory and trade would begin to alter this wholesome balance in the year 1609 on the shores of the lake that bears the name of its European conqueror.

THE EUROPEANS

In 1567, Samuel de Champlain, the son of a French naval captain, was born at Brouage, France. At an early age he showed a dexterity for draftmanship and navigation, and in 1603, at the age of thirty-six, he embarked on the first of twelve voyages to North America. Over the next thirty years, these expeditions would earn him the distinction of the discoverer of the Ottawa River and Lakes Champlain, Ontario, and Huron. They also gave him claim to the titles Founder of Quebec and Father of New France, and he was an adversary of the League of the Iroquois.

The first confrontation between the French and the Iroquois occurred in the spring of 1609, as Champlain gathered a war party of sixty Hurons and Algonquins and two Frenchmen. They started up the lake that now bears his name, in twenty canoes gliding toward the western shore. On July 30, they came upon a war party of approximately two hundred Mohawk. The Mohawk juggernaut, armed with stone and iron axes, resolutely advanced led by two chiefs with large plumed feathers on their headdresses.

The Algonquins and Hurons rushed toward the Mohawk formation and then suddenly parted their ranks in the center. The maneuver revealed Champlain and his fellow Frenchman armed with deadly arquebus. The guns blasted and hit both Mohawk chieftains squarely. The Mohawks had never witnessed firearms in action before. The sight of their fallen leaders, the roar, and the fire and smoke of the firearms was too much for the Mohawks and they fled the field, pursued by Champlain's Indian allies. The Mohawks returned to their villages in the valley with bitterness in their hearts toward the French. Champlain later pompously wrote: "The place where this battle was fought is in 43 degrees, some minutes latitude, and I named it Lake Champlain."[9]

The political and economic rationale for Champlain and other explorers to risk these forays into the land of the Iroquois was driven by two factors—imperial conquest and the fur trade. In the 1600's, the French in North America were locked in a furious trade competition with the Dutch and later the English over the acquisition of valuable animal skins. In seventeenth century Europe, beaver hats and collars were the rage of fashion and there was a scarcity of fur-bearing animals on the continent. There were tremendous profits to be made by trading with the Indians in North America. Goods bought for one livre in New France could be traded for pelts worth two hundred livre when brought back to Paris. The French constructed military posts such as Niagara to protect their burgeoning interests.

As enemies of France, the Iroquois dealt primarily with Dutch traders from the colony of New Netherland at Fort Orange. The Iroquois were very desirous to obtain European goods such as iron kettles, knives, scissors, nails, axes, and woolen clothing to improve their lifestyle. The metal objects were much more durable than the earthen pottery and stone or bone implements which the natives had previously used.

There were several negative consequences of this trend. The Iroquois began to favor the European products so much that they stopped learning traditional skills such as pottery and tool-making. Very rapidly the goods that once seemed luxuries became necessities of life. A Mohawk chieftain expressed his tribe's dilemma in a conversation with Dutch officials in 1659: "The Dutch say we are brothers, and joined together with chains, but that lasts only as long as we have beavers; after that no attention is paid to us."[10]

In a short time, the number of beaver in the land of the Iroquois had dwindled because of over-hunting. The situation became desperate. Without pelts, the people of the Five Nations could not acquire the goods they needed to perform daily activities. The choice was clear—seek new sources of animal skins or face starvation.

The members of the Confederacy initiated a policy of territorial expansion and warfare directed at their Algonquin and Huron neighbors that would eventually take them to the gates of Montreal and the territory of the Illinois. The Iroquois Confederacy was in a geographically favorable position, they were in control of the waterways and were wedged between the French in the north and the Dutch in the east.

The internal unity of the Five Nations, coupled with their military successes, placed them in an important position in the upcoming struggle between European powers as it played out on the North American continent. For a time, the skilled diplomats of the Iroquois would attempt to take full advantage of the opportunity presented to them. The Iroquois would emerge as the most powerful political force on the continent.

In 1664, Great Britain took control of lands claimed by the Dutch in the New World as a result of English victories in both Europe and North America. Shortly thereafter, New Netherland became New York and Fort Orange was renamed Albany. In the same year Mohawk and Seneca representatives concluded a commercial agreement with British merchants, pledging to shift their allegiance to the Crown.

However, new hostilities developed as British settlers moved into Mohawk territory. The settlers did not always deal fairly with the natives in negotiating land deals. In one case, two Mohawks were tricked into signing a deed granting an Englishman control over an enormous area, extending fifty miles on both sides of the Mohawk River west of Albany. This fraud was brought to light and the deed annulled, but many other bogus deals went undetected.

Matters concerning land or trade were not the only areas of conflict between the Iroquois and Europeans. There were also cultural clashes between the two groups.

Beginning in the 1640's, French Jesuit missionaries had begun working among the Indians of North America. The story of Father Isaac Jogues is typical of their experience. Isaac Jogues was born in Orleans, France in 1607, was ordained into the Society of Jesus in 1624, and began his missionary work among the Hurons in 1636. In 1642, he was captured and taken to the land of the Mohawks. He escaped with the help of the Dutch, but during the next four years, waves of disease brought by the Europeans killed hundreds of the Indians. Crops had also failed in this same time period. The Mohawks assigned blame to a black box which had been left by Jogues.

When he returned to their village in 1646 as an ambassador of the French government, Bear Clan leaders executed Jogues in spite of the opposition of the Wolf and Turtle Clans. In 1930, the Roman Catholic Church canonized Father Jogues along with seven other Jesuit martyrs of North America.

Another Jesuit priest later to be martyred, Father Gabriel Lalemant, had observed: "It is true that, speaking humanly, these Barbarians have apparent reasons for reproaching us—inasmuch as the scourges which humble the proud precede us or accompany us wherever we go."[11]

The English also would make misguided attempts to "edify the savages." In 1744, commissioners from Maryland and Virginia invited the Iroquois to send twelve Indian boys to the College of William and Mary for a formal education. The chieftain, Conassatego, sent this response:

> "We are convinced that you mean to do us good by your proposal, and we thank you heartily. But you, who are wise must know that different nations have different conceptions of things and you will not therefore take it amiss, if our ideas of this kind of education happen not to be the same as yours.
>
> We have had some experience of it. Several of our young people were formerly brought up at the colleges of the northern provinces, where they were instructed in your sciences; But, when they came back they were bad runners, ignorant of every means of living in the woods... neither fit for hunters, warriors, nor counsellors... They were totally good for nothing.

We are, however, not the less obliged by your kind offer, tho' we decline accepting it; and to show our grateful sense of it, if the gentlemen of Virginia will send us a dozen of their sons, we will take care of their education, instruct them in all we know, and make men of them."[12]

In 1715, at the Manor of Killeen near Warrenstown, County Meath, Ireland, a baby boy was born who would measure up to the Iroquois definition of a man, and the destiny of the people of the Five Nations would forever be transformed because of him.

The Confederacy of the Five Nations, from Hubbards' *Red Jacket and His People*, collection of the Oneida County Historical Society

"Her child should be a son whom she should name 'Peacemaker'," from Collins' *The Story of America in Pictures*, collection of Fred Reed

"On the sixth day Hayonwatha rested," from Parker's *The Iroquois*, collection of the Oneida County Historical Society

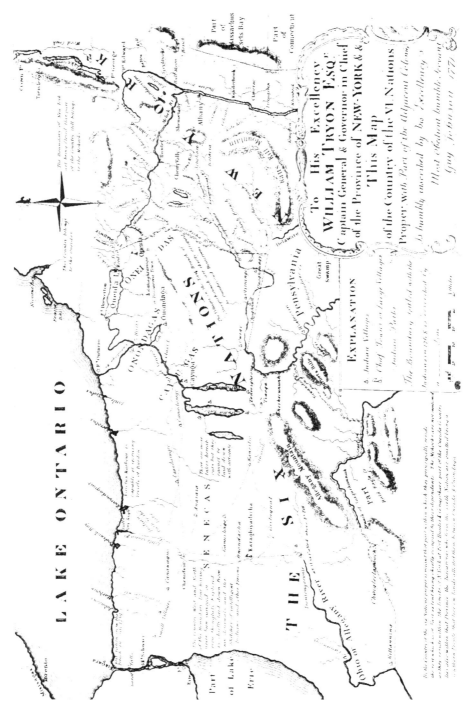

Map of the Six Nations, 1771, from Adams' *The Longhouse of the Iroquois*, collection of the Oneida County Historical Society

The interior of an Iroquois longhouse, from Greene's *The Mohawk Valley*

Harvest time, from Greene's *The Mohawk Valley*

The Battle of Lake Champlain, from Collins' *The Story of America in Pictures*, collection of Fred Reed

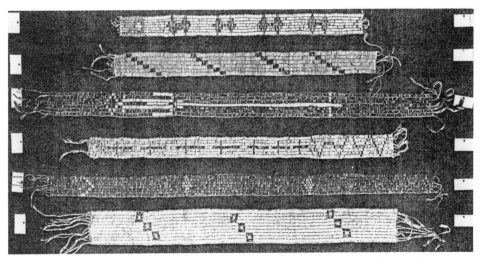

Wampum, from Adams' *The Longhouse of the Iroquois*, collection of the Oneida County Historical Society

A fur trader negotiates with some Indians, from Greene's *The Mohawk Valley*

Jesuit missionaries preaching to the Iroquois, from Collins' *The Story of America in Pictures*, collection of Fred Reed

If I should die, think only this of me:
That there's some corner of a foreign field
That is forever England
                              —*Rupert Brooke*

Chapter Three

THE LOYALISTS

Statue of Sir William Johnson, courtesy of New York State Office of Parks, Recreation, and Historic Preservation, Johnson Hall State Historic Site

A FUNERAL PROCESSION

The great man was dead. Sir William Johnson, knight of the realm and baronet of the Mohawk Valley, had finally succumbed to the illness brought on by years of rich living and excessive drinking, cirrhosis of the liver.

On July 11, 1774, because of one more frontier crisis, Warraghiyagey, as he was known by his dear friends the Iroquois, found it necessary to rise from his sick bed and address the assembled sachem and six hundred of their followers. In the hot summer sun, in an arbor behind his splendid home at Johnson Hall, he tottered on weak legs. Sir William gave the attentive warriors, squaws, and children one last directive in the looming shadow of conflict: "Whatever may happen, you must not be shaken out of your shoes."[1]

He then ordered some "pipes, tobacco, and liquor" for his native allies and, with assistance, retired to his chambers. He gulped some water and wine, slumped into a chair, and with his head back, sighed his last breath. He left an empire encompassing land grants of almost ninety-three thousand acres and a powerful political influence extending much farther.

The funeral procession slowly wove its way down the long hill from Johnson Hall to St. John's Episcopal Church in Johnstown. First came all the principal clergymen of the region. Next was the coffin bearing the body of the sixty-year-old lord. The mourning cloth covering the casket, though tacked down with silver nails, flapped in the breeze. Sir William's remains were carried on the shoulders of some well-recognized names of New York colonial society including Robert Morris, Robert Livingston, and Gov. William Franklin of New Jersey.

Next in the column came the great man's heirs. While some were children of his contrived marriage to Catherine Weissenberg, most were from his many affairs. Leading this mixed assortment of individuals was Sir John Johnson, who had wasted no time in already invoking his new title as "Baronet." The thirty-two-year-old Sir John was the first born son of Catherine, a young German indentured servant acquired from a valley neighbor, whom Sir William repeatedly welcomed to his bed. The accommodating maid also presented her master with two daughters. According to some accounts, "Lord" Johnson finally got around to the formality of marrying housekeeper Catherine on her deathbed to authenticate their children as his heirs.

In a bid for royal recognition of John's right of succession and to smooth his rustic country edges, Sir William had sent his son to England in 1765. To the baronet's immense relief, George III immediately bestowed a knighthood upon him. The demure young aristocrat did not win over English society as easily. A former visitor to Johnson Hall, Lord Gordon, lamented, "His modesty conceals his merit."[2]

Unlike his father, Sir John was short, slender, and blond and had a round effeminate face with petite lips puckered above a receding chin. It was hardly an appearance to command the attention and confidence of people. His developing persona would not have any of the charismatic characteristics of Sir William.

The homesick young lord soon departed for the "sweet, enchanting banks of the Mohawk," with a newly acquired English butler and coachman in tow. Soon after his return, and like his father before him, he set up residence in Fort Johnson in the company of a comely lover, Clarissa Putnam of a German Episcopal family. This union produced two illegitimate offspring, a son William Johnson II and a daughter Margaret.

The frustrated Sir William implored his son to find a more suitable wife, realizing that titles and property could not be expected to be passed on to a continual line of illegitimate heirs. In 1773, Sir John finally relented by sending Clarissa and the two children into exile and marrying the rich New York debutante Polly Watts.

The trappings of a British education and the titles bestowed upon him changed his personality so as to cause the valley population to feel less warmth toward him than his popular father. The young man became arrogant and took on an assumption of superiority. He began to look upon his humble and religious neighbors along the river as not being worthy enough to associate with him, a knight and baronet of the realm of Great Britain. His weak character would prevent him from exerting the same measure of influence that his father did over the inhabitants of Tryon County, white or Indian. In the end, he was not interested in the responsibilities of his position, only in the trappings of his title.

In a few short years, Sir John would be motivated by a different destructive human emotion, revenge. It would be a vengeance of catastrophic proportions wreaked upon many of his former neighbors in the valley of the Mohawk.

Following Sir John in the funeral train were his two grieving sisters and their spouses. Sir William's younger daughter, Mary, had married her cousin Guy Johnson, the baronet's nephew. Guy had shown up unexpectedly at Fort Johnson in 1756, a rather coarse Irish lad of sixteen. He was welcomed by his uncle with open arms and given a commission in the militia in lieu of any formal education. As Sir William was pleased with his daughter's marriage to Guy, the Mohawk Valley lord built for the couple a fine mansion near Fort Johnson named Guy Park. Upon the death of Sir

William, Guy Johnson would be appointed Superintendent of Indian Affairs by the Crown. Like his cousin John, the jovial and fun-loving Guy would have a difficult time equaling the intense loyalty of his Iroquois brethren gained by Sir William.

Sir William's elder daughter by Catherine Weissenberg, Ann, was married to Daniel Claus. Claus was an emigre from Wurttemberg who had come to Philadelphia to seek his fortune and fame. In 1754, the Royal Government of Pennsylvania sent Claus to the Mohawk Valley to learn Indian speech and ways. Taking a liking to the young man, a fondness which was mutual, the baronet "kidnapped" Claus into his own service. For several years, Claus held his love and admiration for Lady Ann close to his vest until such time as Sir William promised help to advance his career. Claus carefully prepared a letter to his employer in which he requested a loan of eight hundred pounds so that he could obtain a commission in the regular British army and "secure a genteel certainty for life."[3] He then concluded the letter by requesting permission for Ann's hand in marriage.

Next in the entourage of the great man's kinsmen came the proud "Brown Mrs. Johnson," Molly Brant (Degonwadonti). His Mohawk mistress of eighteen years and the greatest love of his life, she would bear eight of the baronet's offspring. Molly Brant was not simply a child of the wilderness. She was Indian royalty. Her grandfather Brant (Sagayeeanquarashtow) had been one of the four Indian chieftains to visit Queen Anne in London and her father was one of the leading sachems of the Mohawk tribe. From her mother's lineage, she was equally ennobled with the title "elder sister of the Mohawk nation."

According to Iroquois ritual, she was married to Warraghiyagey and from the time she was about sixteen years of age, he laid by her side as befitting an Iroquois brave. While in her village Sir William spoke Mohawk, and in his parlor Molly wore her Indian clothes. Molly lived in William's white world without allowing it to influence her native customs. Their children were raised in the Indian tradition.

Degonwadonti gave Warraghiyagey his space while maintaining her own integrity. She ignored his dalliances with beautiful squaws and farmers' daughters. She concealed her own secrets and feelings. She was imbued with a serenity and nobility which mesmerized the worldly Johnson. She spoke with a fire that charmed and heated his own passion.

At Johnson Hall, Molly Brant dominated the household with authority. She occupied two of the backrooms on the ground floor as a bedroom and nursery. Unlike Sir William's previous mistresses, she refused to yield any prestige to younger beauties over the years. It appears that the baronet had finally met his equal. She would sometimes join him on military campaigns and, of course, was an invaluable asset to him in his constant dealings with the Five Nations. Sir William's relationship with Molly Brant symbolized his special bond with the Iroquois people and, consequently, he monitored their interests with the colonial and royal authorities closely.

Late in Sir William's life, when he was often plagued by illness, it was Molly who often parlayed with the endless delegations of Indian diplomats who came to Johnson Hall, thus helping shape official Indian policy. In tribute to her, Sir William allowed her to play hostess to his white guests as well, always insisting that she be treated politely.

Striding behind Molly were her eight children by Sir William. After them, came Brant Johnson and William Johnson of Canajoharie. These were two more of the baronet's illegitimate sons by an earlier relationship with another Iroquois maiden, reputed to be Caroline, niece of the great Mohawk sachem Hendrick.

There poured down the slope a vast multitude of Mohawk chiefs, warriors, women, and children who had come to pay tribute to their fallen comrade, followed by two thousand loyal valley settlers. The other tribes of the Five Nations were also well represented.

Within five years most of those who slowly descended the hill to the tolling of the funeral bell would themselves be dead or exiled from their hearths and homes.

AN IRISHMAN COMES TO AMERICA

In early 1738, a young William Johnson joined his uncle, Peter Warren, in Boston. The twenty-three-year-old son of Peter's sister, Anne, had received an invitation from his uncle to recruit Irish peasants to build a plantation in the Mohawk Valley on Warren's land in exchange for ship's passage. William was to oversee the project as Warren's agent. Among the lad's duties would be to cultivate a farm with servants and slaves, lease land to settlers, and establish a store for these tenants.

William was under the impression that his uncle meant to give him a generous boost in the new world and anticipated that the farm was intended to be his. Peter, on the other hand, expected that his poor relation would be grateful for any scraps of favor thrown to him and sorely underestimated the mettle of this raw Irish youth. Within three bustling years the valley estate which had at first been grandly dubbed Warrensburg became known as Mount Johnson.

The British military outpost, Fort Hunter, was nearby and overlooked the Lower Mohawk Castle. Young William was fascinated by the Iroquois braves who frequently traded at the fort, and who were decoratively painted and greased with bear fat. This was the beginning of his long entrancement with the people of the Five Nations.

Johnson had brought twelve families with him who had been recruited from County Meath. They joined the eight tenants of primarily German stock already on the Warrensburg property. More refugees from the Palatinate (region in Germany) were to follow. It was from this sturdy folk that William would choose as his mistress, Catherine Weissenberg.

With clear vision, William Johnson saw the waters of his Mohawk River flowing westward toward expansion. He understood the strategic importance of the valley in the ongoing jostling for influence and land between the French and British. Recognizing the importance of the Iroquois League in this continuing struggle, he curried favor with their leaders and consolidated colonial authority for himself.

He set up neighbors in the fur trade and attracted the attention of the Indian trappers by consistently outbidding the traders at Forts Oswego and Albany. He adopted a policy of what he called "fair dealing with the settlers."[4] In return for his acts of kindness he expected loyalty, and he received it. He considered the settlers and his Iroquois neighbors as clan brothers whose economic prosperity was irrevocably intertwined with his own well being.

CHAMPION OF THE IROQUOIS

Most important to his future success was the relationship that began to develop between Johnson and the grand political strategist of the Mohawk nation, King Hendrick (Tiyanoga). Hendrick was one of the "Four Indian Kings" who had visited London in 1710 at the invitation of Queen Anne. He would regale Johnson, who had never been there, with tales of this gem of a city "with streets as long as rivers," and speak of the royal queen who had touched his hand. A contemporary declared that King Hendrick "appeared as if born to command, and possessed a majesty unrivaled."[5]

Like Johnson's white tenants, the Indians needed a champion to represent their needs to the English authorities. Johnson took on the task, mastering the difficult Mohawk language. The developing affection between Johnson and the Indians culminated with Johnson being officially adopted as a Mohawk as prescribed by Gayanashagowa or The Great Binding Law. The Mohawks renamed Johnson "Warraghiyagey," meaning "a man who undertakes great things." And great tests were coming for Warraghiyagey, courtesy of the rival French and their Indian allies.

KING GEORGE'S WAR

In 1744, the colonies were notified that England was officially at war with France as the War of the Austrian Succession had begun in Europe.

New York's royal governor, Sir George Clinton, was given the task of carrying out military policy, but was met with some foot-dragging on the part of the New York Assembly and the declared neutrality of the Iroquois League.

A thin line of settlements buried in the forest was a poor defensible position in the Mohawk Valley and Johnson moved to fortify Mount Johnson as best he could. He secured a brass cannon and some swivels from his uncle, Peter Warren. His presence was a source of comfort to the settlers and Mohawks, fearful of French raids, who knew that Johnson stayed in spite of a standing invitation to flee to Albany.

In recognition of William Johnson's unique status with the Iroquois, Governor Clinton appointed him Indian Commissioner in 1746. Later, through the jealousy and political maneuvering of Massachusetts Governor William Shirley, he was forced to resign this post. The subsequent uproar from the Iroquois quickly rescinded the decision. At the age of thirty-one, after only eight years of personal empire building, Johnson was in a position powerful enough to defy even royal governors.

It was Commissioner Johnson that offered the only hope for Clinton, now based in Albany, to carry out His Majesty's command for an attack on Canada. On a dry evening in July of 1746, he entered the Mohawk Castle of Teantontaloga and went into one of the lodges of his Indian compatriots. Johnson put on "moccasins, a kilt of deerskins embroidered with porcupine quills, and a feather-tufted skull cap bound with a silver band and crowned with a great eagle feather. He painted designs on his naked torso and attached to his arms, his wrists, and his knees rattles of dried deer hooves that shook with a crackling rustle."

From the lodge there arose the same war cry that had signaled to the Iroquois for centuries that the time for battle had come. Johnson chanted to the warriors of the power of King George and about the great army that would come to assist the Five Nations in casting their ancestral enemies, the French and their Indian allies, into oblivion. The Iroquois needed only a modicum of encouragement.

The Iroquois remembered that, in 1689, the Mohawk leader, Tahajadoris, had responded to a request from the English colonists for assistance against the Abenakis and French in this way, "We patiently bore many injuries from the French, from one year to another. We assure you that we are resolved never to drop the axe; the French shall never see our faces in peace, we shall never be reconciled as long as one Frenchman is alive."[6]

With the hammering of drums and approving shouts of the Mohawk braves ringing in his ears, Warraghiyagey drove a red-painted hatchet into the war post. One after another, the various sachem threw off their blankets and joined the frenzied war dance. They were "...one flesh, one heart, one brain...."

In August of 1746, residents of Albany rushed from their homes to stare at a most unusual sight. Mohawk braves, stripped to the waist and brightly decorated with war paint, tramped single file through the streets, shouting their battle cries. They were led by William Johnson, the wild-eyed Irishman from County Meath, similarly half-naked and adorned.

They approached the fort where His Majesty's royal governor leaned over the ramparts gazing in awe. As he reached the wall of the bastion, Johnson fired his musket into the ground. Every Mohawk brave who followed did the same, as Clinton's cannon roared a reply in salute. Out of the desolate wilderness had stepped a man determined to carve a niche for himself in history, and on the carcass's of his king's enemies if necessary.

The congress of Iroquois and English opened on August 19, 1746. An English orator spoke of a "Covenant Chain" to "bind them forever in Brothership together, and that your warriors and ours should be as one heart, one head, one blood..." and the governor ordered "that should this silver chain turn the least rusty, offer to slip or break, that it should immediately be brightened up again, and not let it slip or break an any account, for then you and we were both dead. Brethren, these are the words of our forefathers, which some among you know very well to be so."[7]

After a four day conference of the Iroquois leaders, the English received their response: "We are now heartily entered into the war with you." The governor appointed William Johnson "Colonel of the forces to be raised out of the Six Nations." (The Tuscarora had joined the Iroquois Confederacy in 1710, having been adopted en masse by the Oneidas.)

In the spring of 1747, a war party of twenty-three braves under the command of Lt. Walter Butler Jr., hid on a hill observing the activity of the enemy at Crown Point. Descending the hill, they crept under an embankment and surprised a small detachment of French soldiers and Indians.

In the ensuing skirmish, they dispatched a number of the enemy to their eternal rest, taking six scalps in the process. Johnson was pleased that a force under his supervision had performed so admirably. He wrote, "This is esteemed the gallantest action performed by the Indians since the commencement of the present war."[8]

Johnson both dreaded and lusted for the fierce conflict taking place in the dense woods. Iroquois raiders brought scalps and prisoners to his doorsteps. The border raids that Johnson initiated had closed the door of trade with Canada. Whatever animal furs that reached the colony of New York now had to come through the colonel's Iroquois-controlled Mohawk Valley route. He thus gained a virtual monopoly on the most lucrative trade item in North America. Warraghiyagey garnered additional clout when Governor Clinton made him the Superintendent of Indian Affairs at Hendrick's insistence.

PEACE AND PROSPERITY

In October of 1748, King George's War, as it was called in North America, came to an official end with the signing of the Peace of Aix-la-Chapelle. Colonel Johnson built a stone house in 1749, later to be known as Fort Johnson. In August of 1749, he was entrusted by Governor Clinton with the delicate mission of handling the exchange of war prisoners between the Six Nations and the French. He successfully concluded this with zeal, energy, and masterful diplomacy. For the next six years a period of peace and prosperity showered the Mohawk Valley. The population at this time numbered about 2,500.

There was considerable building activity in the valley in 1750 and a number of homes and churches were erected. Johannes Klock built Fort Klock and Fort Wagner was constructed by Johan Peter Wagner. These structures were palisaded for purposes of defense during the American Revolution. Martin Van Alstyne came to the site of the present village of Canajoharie and built a stone house on his property near the creek. There he kept a tavern which would later become a favorite meeting place of the Tryon County Committee of Safety. Several old houses in Schenectady also date from this period of development.

Early in 1754, the English House of Lords directed the royal colonial governors to send delegates to an American colonial congress which would make a treaty of friendship and alliance with the Indian tribes. Seven colonies complied and the congress commenced in Albany on June 29. The influence of Sir William and his close friend Mohawk sachem Hendrick brought about the attendance of a number of important chiefs of the Six Nations.

King Hendrick promised that the Iroquois would firmly hold the covenant chain, but that the British had neglected their Indian allies and that many people of the Six Nations were starving. Johnson prepared a plan for the proper management of the Six Nations, which was taken home by the delegates to their respective colonial governments for consideration. Through Johnson's influence, the Iroquois allegiance was maintained.

During the six years of peace, the Mohawk Valley prospered. Recent immigrant settlers had doubled the population to over 5,000. Settlements were growing at a rapid pace, attracted by William Johnson's stellar status in the colony of New York and by the plentiful and fertile land. Sir William's dominating fingers of influence were spreading in all directions.

THE FRENCH AND INDIAN WAR

The peace would be shattered by a sequence of events beginning in 1753. The new governor general of Canada, the Marquis Duquesne, sent an expedition of one thousand men to build a series of three forts in the region of the Ohio Valley. One of these was Fort Le Boeuf. Lt. Gov. Robert Dinwiddie of Virginia sent a solemn warning to Legardeur de Saint Pierre, commandant of Fort Le Boeuf, accusing the French of trespassing on the domain of His Majesty. It stated, "Lands on the Ohio River to the West of the Colony of Virginia belong properly to the Crown of Great Britain." Duquesne countered, "Our King wants it, and that is enough to march ahead."[9] It was clear that the issues were beyond the stage of peaceful resolution.

By 1754, undeclared warfare was breaking out all across the northern frontier. The British initially suffered two serious setbacks. First, the capture by the French of a fort being erected by Virginia traders and backwoodsmen on the Ohio River. Secondly, the twenty-two-year-old colonel of the Virginia militia, George Washington, and his regiment were defeated at the hastily erected Fort Necessity. The French and Indian War had begun.

In 1755, Gen. Edward Braddock was placed in command of His Majesty's forces in North America and arrived with two regiments of British regulars and the authority to raise two additional regiments in the colonies. In April, Braddock met with the royal governors of several colonies to develop a strategic plan for the upcoming campaign.

Four expeditions were decided upon. The first, commanded by Col. Robert Monckton with two thousand New England troops, was to capture Fort Beausejour, bring the Acadians into submission, and prepare the fort as a jumping off point for a siege of the fortress city of Louisburg.

The second, led by Braddock himself, was to march against Fort Duquesne, seize it and then pivot for an attack against Fort Niagara. The third, commanded by Governor Shirley of Massachusetts, after a rendevous in Schenectady, was to proceed up the Mohawk River, cross the Lake of the Oneidas, go down the Oswego River to Fort Oswego and from there assault Fort Frontenac on the north shore of Lake Ontario and then assist Braddock at Niagara.

The fourth contingent was led by newly appointed General of Militia, William Johnson, gathering an army at Albany and then proceeding northward for an attack on Fort St. Frederic at Crown Point and an occupation of this vicinity.

The first three expeditions met with disaster. Fort Beausejour capitulated to Monckton on June 16, but the stubborn Acadians refused to take the oath of allegiance to his Brittanic Majesty. Braddock began his march through the wilderness to Fort Duquesne and, on July 9, 1755, he and his column of British regulars and Virginia militia were ambushed and horribly defeated within ten miles of the fort. The general died four days later from a wound he had received during the ambush.

General Johnson's old rival Governor Shirley and his troops started up the Mohawk River in early July. After crossing Oneida Lake, Shirley learned of Braddock's defeat. From this point on, he began to slow his advance, finally rumbling to a halt one month later at Oswego. Knowing that the pincer movement against Fort Niagara was now impossible, Shirley put his men to work strengthening the fort while he scurried back to Albany to make excuses for his lack of progress. It now remained with General Johnson and his men to salvage the military fortunes of the Crown in North America.

Johnson and three thousand militiamen from New York, Massachusetts, New Hampshire, and Rhode Island began the advance north from Albany. Later they were joined by approximately two hundred Mohawk braves including Johnson's loyal friend Hendrick, now old, plump, and requiring a horse.

THE BATTLE OF LAKE GEORGE

At 4:00 in the afternoon on August 28, 1755, Johnson's advance column arrived at the lake the French called St. Sacrament. In a letter to the House of Lords, General Johnson announced, "I am building a fort at this lake... I have given it the name of Lake George not only in honor of His Majesty but to ascertain his undoubted dominion here."[10]

Under the direction of Col. Ephraim Williams (founder of Williams College), the erection of the fort began on September 7. That same afternoon, Johnson's Indian scouts reported the movement of a large body of white men and Indians traveling toward them. This proved to be a French army of fifteen hundred under the command of Baron Dieskau, a well-trained soldier who had earned his merits on the battlefields of Europe under Marshall Saxe. The baron was attempting to surprise Johnson's forces in the rear where his defenses were unfortified.

General Johnson called a council of war with his officers at which various tactical options were discussed. At first, plans were made to divide the troops into three sections. One to remain at the head of the lake, the second to march eastward, the third to march southward over the military road. King Hendrick, who normally attended these sessions, but rarely spoke, immediately arose and without saying a word, took three sticks and snapped each one in two separately. He then took three more sticks and grasping them together, he failed to break them. After showing them the folly of their plan, he quietly sat down.

It was finally agreed that half the manpower would march back along the military road in an attempt to locate the enemy under the command of Colonel Williams, with his second being Colonel Whiting. After hearing of this decision, King Hendrick sadly shook his head and spoke to Johnson in Mohawk, "If they are to die, they are too many; if they are to fight, they are too few."[11]

Ephraim Williams's one thousand-man "scouting party" moved out at 8:00 A.M. on September 8, 1755. He ordered the Mohawks to scout ahead of the main body. These Indians looked to Hendrick for directions. Turning to Williams, Hendrick muttered in English, "I smell Indians." He whispered something to his braves in Mohawk, motioned with his left hand, and they melted into the underbrush.

A herd of deer sprinted across a gully to the east of the column, up ahead crows circled and cackled a warning. None of these signals gave any of the American officers a premonition, only Hendrick slouched in his saddle in resignation.

Williams looked back at the column and was in the process of waving them forward when the forest belched fire. The front of the column reeled back in chaos as both Williams' and King Hendrick's horses went down. The colonel extricated himself from his prone stallion and, drawing his sword, urged the soldiers to move up a slope to the west. A horseshoe shaped ambush had enveloped the advance elements of the formation. The Abenaki warriors and French regulars pressed their advantage. The Mohawks who had been ordered by Hendrick to scout the woods held their own in skirmish formation, hiding behind trees, firing their muskets, and pausing only to reload and chide their attackers.

As Colonel Williams leapt onto a rock to rally his troops, he was shot clean through the head and instantly struck dead. In Johnson's camp, the disposition of the battle was all too evident, and he ordered the wagons and bateaux drawn up to form a semi-circular wall. Eventually Whiting's rear guard and the survivors of the main body emerged from the forest, hurrying for the entrenchments.

There was one other casualty in particular who bears mentioning in this engagement: This part of the battle would be remembered as the "Bloody Morning Scout."

King Hendrick had been trapped under his fallen horse, unable to free himself; he was roughly bayoneted by a French regular. After the smoke of battle had dissipated, Johnson went in search of his old friend. He found him where he had fallen. Johnson openly wept over the bloodstained body. The great Iroquois diplomat was forever silenced.

Behind their barricades the American colonials fixed bayonets and took swigs of rum. From the forest came the crackling sound of Baron Dieskau's regulars, Canadians, and Indians advancing toward them. The baron paraded his regulars down the center, just out of musket range, preparing for the main assault with his Canadian militia and Indians on the flanks in support. The phalanx of men surged forward, firing by platoon. General Johnson received a musket ball in the leg in the very first volley. He turned over command to General Lyman and retired to his tent.

The American artillery took a deadly toll of the French regulars, cutting them down in swaths. Seeing his frontal assault failing, Dieskau attempted to turn first one flank of the colonials and then the other, but was met by determined resistance. As the baron regrouped his troops for one final push, he was shot down by two musket balls.

After four hours of see-saw battle, General Lyman, sword in hand, motioned the troops to charge. In seemingly one motion, the Americans swept over their ramparts and began to butcher the French with the business end of their bayonets and the swinging chop of their tomahawks. The baron, lying prostrate on the ground, barely escaped death and was taken prisoner by a New Englander.

The English victory was complete in this engagement remembered as "The Battle of Bloody Pond." The bodies of the slain enemy were unceremoniously dumped into a nearby pond, the blood coloring the water a deep red in the reflection of the setting sun. The raw colonial militia had proven itself against a force of European arms.

On November 8, 1755, Gen. William Johnson issued orders from his headquarters in the newly proclaimed Fort William Henry, named after a grandson of George II. On November 27, Johnson and his victorious army were relieved by replacement troops and marched to Fort Edward where they were discharged.

In January 1756, William Johnson became Sir William Johnson, Baronet. He was granted this title for his service to the Crown during the Battle of Lake George. Great Britain added to this lustre a gift of five thousand pounds, which Sir William prudently invested in the Bank of England.

Sir William would serve his country ably again by his forthright action at the fall of Fort Niagara in 1759, perhaps one of the greatest English military victories during the French and Indian War. By 1761, the war had sputtered to a close and England had significantly added to her territorial sovereignty.

EMERGENCE OF A MOHAWK LEADER

In the summer of 1761, a special messenger rode up to the fortified door of Sir William Johnson's home in the valley. He carried a letter from Parson Eleazar Wheelock. The parson ran a free school for Indians in Lebanon, Connecticut. Some day this same school would move to New Hampshire and change its name to Dartmouth College.

The letter said in part that, "The honorable commissioners of the Society in Scotland for propagating Christian knowledge have granted a support for three boys of the Six Nations at the school under my care in order to their being fitted as soon as may be for interpreters or other public usefulness among their own Nations...." Sir William had been recommended to Wheelock by Johnson's comrade-in-arms from the Lake George campaign, Connecticut Gen. Phineas Lyman, as being best able to judge the suitable candidates for this opportunity.

Johnson selected two boys of the Wolf Clan of the Mohawk Nation named Sander and Nickus, both of whom were veterans of the Montreal campaign and recipients of Lord Jeffery Amherst's silver medals.

For his third choice, he nominated the eighteen-year-old younger brother of Molly Brant, Joseph, also known as "Thayendanegea." Wheelock noted that Joseph came better dressed, could already speak a little English, and apparently had Sir William's high regard. This affection was not without merit.

More so than any of Sir William's natural born sons, Joseph Brant would develop the leadership qualities akin to Johnson's own skills that would have the power to stir a nation to action. In many ways, Thayendanegea would become the logical heir to Sir William's wilderness domain. At the youthful age of eighteen he was already described as "a sprightly genius, with a manly and genteel disposition, and a modest, courteous, benevolent temper."[12]

As was his mentor, Thayendanegea was also a man of two worlds. He "carried a sword in one hand and the prayer book in the other." He used his profound eloquence to move the Indian councils as well as white assemblies.

In November of 1761, Joseph returned home from school for a short visit. His traveling companion was a fellow white student named Samuel Kirkland. Kirkland was planning to become a missionary and was struggling to learn the difficult Mohawk language. Brant, who approved of Christian education, was pleased to assist him as they journeyed together. In later years, Thayendanegea may have recalled this gesture of kindness with regret. For Samuel Kirkland also would possess the talent for straddling two worlds, white and Indian, with tragic consequences for the Iroquois Confederacy.

JOHNSON HALL

By 1755, Sir William had begun to plan a new settlement to be known as Johnstown and, in 1761, began construction of a grand new estate which he called Johnson Hall. By 1763, he had relocated his household to this place. Johnson Hall was a frame building, sixty feet long, forty feet wide and two stories high, facing a neighboring creek to the southeast. Slightly to the rear of the main structure were two stone blockhouses built as part of the defenses of the Hall. Today the estate still stands as a state-owned museum.

Sir William's favorite room was the blue parlor, in which hung the prints of the British king, queen, and royal family. Across the hall was the white parlor which doubled as a dining room. As previously mentioned, he shared the two back rooms with Molly Brant. The kitchen and the butler's room were in the cellar. Other servants were housed in the huge attic.

The four rooms on the second floor were reserved for guests. Into these chambers poured visitors from "all parts of America, Europe and the West Indies." Sir William spared no expense in hospitality. Guests would breakfast in their respective bedrooms on tea, coffee, or chocolate, accompanied by a beef steak and a mug of ale for those with heartier appetites.

Daily entertainment included shooting, fishing, breezing through town, or playing cards, backgammon, billiards, or nine pins. Promptly at four o'clock in the afternoon, the dinner bell rang and the ten to thirty guests plus Johnson's own large family would assemble for a sumptuous feast of venison, bear, fish, wild turkey, partridge, grouse, or quail in great abundance. The liquor flowed freely including Madeira, ale, hard cider, and wine punch.

The festivities sometimes included an Irish harper or fiddler, and a number of the Indian sachems would often join in the mirth and merriment which usually went on into the wee hours of the morning. Among the more frequent visitors was a physician named Richard Shuckbaugh, who much preferred drinking to doctoring. In 1765, he had set to music a little ditty mocking the New England militia called "Yankee Doodle." Life was good for Sir William Johnson and his settlement in the Mohawk Valley.

Fifteen years before the arrival of William Johnson in America, there came to the Mohawk Valley a group of settlers whose descendants would form the nucleus of another American militia brigade. They seemed a haughty lot, but this only disguised a suspicious nature conditioned by repeated hardship and betrayal. Snobs of Loyalist sentiment would rue the day they ridiculed such determined folk. They were the Palatines.

Sir John Johnson, courtesy of New York State Office of Parks, Recreation, and Historic Preservation, Johnson Hall State Historic Site

Daniel Claus, collection of the Montgomery County
Historical Society

Molly Brant, artist's rendering by John Mahaffy

Hendrick, collection of the Montgomery County Historical Society

Statue of Sir William and King Hendrick, *American Heritage* magazine, Spring 1952

Joseph Brant, from Reid's *Old Fort Johnson*

William Johnson, collection of the Montgomery County
Historical Society

Johnson Hall, from Simms' *Trappers of New York*, collection of the Utica Public Library

Photo by the author

At the Battle of Lake George, "The Americans swept over the ramparts," collection of Joseph Robertaccio

Bring me men to match my mountains
Bring me men to match my plains
Men with empires in their purpose
And new eras in their brains.
—*S.W. Foss*

Chapter Four

THE PATRIOTS

Statue of Brig. Gen. Nicholas Herkimer, from Greene's *The Mohawk Valley*.

THE PALATINATE

On the banks of a sprawling river with majestic hills in the distance were several well-populated industrious towns nestled in a luxurious fertile valley. Contained in its hamlets and cities were great institutions of learning and worship. One could draw the conclusion that the preceding describes the Mohawk Valley in the nineteenth and twentieth centuries. It is also a fitting image for the region of the Rhine Valley in Germany which was known in the seventeenth century as the "Palatinate," or Pfalz.

The name "Palatinate" comes from the title of a Roman official, a "Palatine," sent by Caesar to govern the southwestern portion of the Holy Roman Empire of German Nation (800-1806) after the conquest of Gaul. From 1225 to 1720, its capital city was Heidelberg, where portions of the castle of the Electors of Palatine still stand. The city is home to its famous namesake, Heidelberg University, founded in 1386, which became a center of Calvinist theology during the Reformation.

Other major population centers in the Palatinate included Mannheim, established in 1606 as a market center and fortified bastion by the Elector of Palatine Frederick IV, and Worms, the site of a diet in 1521 where Martin Luther defended his reformist beliefs before Emperor Charles V.

The issue of religion would be a major factor in a period of armed conflict stretching intermittently across ninety-six years and three major wars. The final outcome hurtled thousands of Palatine refugees to an exodus ultimately ending in their rendezvous with destiny in the valley of the Mohawk.

The religious wars that had divided the Holy Roman Empire of German Nation were renewed with the outbreak of the Thirty Years' War in 1618. On May 23, a number of bohemian Protestant noblemen threw two royal governors out the windows of the Hradcany Palace in Prague to protest the rigid catholic policies of their king, Ferdinand of Hapsburg. Both sides believed they were fighting for a holy cause and feared not only defeat but complete annihilation.

In 1623, the Palatinate was overrun by Spanish and Bavarian troops. The region was devastated and it is estimated that up to fifty percent of the civilian population was put to death. The horrors of the conflict exceeded anything in people's memory until the First and Second World Wars. More deprivation was still to follow.

On July 9, 1686, the League of Augsburg was formed by Holy Roman Emperor Leopold I, several German princes, and the kings of Spain and Sweden. The purpose of the league was to form a defensive alliance to stand against the expansionist yearnings of France under Louis XIV, the "Sun King."

Louis had long coveted the rich lands of the Rhine Valley. In 1685, he had revoked the right of the French Protestant minority to worship with his Edict of Fontainbleau, forcing them to leave the country. Using the excuse that the Palatines harbored some of the persecuted French Huguenots, the despotic ruler ordered French armies to invade the Palatinate in 1688; thus initiating the War of the Grand Alliance.

The royal command dictated that during the French retreat "the Palatinate should be made a desert." Macaulay writes: "The French commander announced to nearly one-half million human beings that he granted them three days of grace, and that within that time they must shift for themselves. Soon the roads and fields, which then lay deep in snow, were blackened by innumerable men, women and children, fleeing from their homes. Many died of cold and hunger, but enough survived to fill the streets of all the cities of Europe with lean and squalid beggars, who had once been thriving farmers and shopkeepers."[1]

Constant wars gave no hope to a people reduced to dire poverty and thousands of the Palatines fled into northern Germany and Holland. Hundreds of towns and villages lay in ashes.

During the War of the Spanish Succession (1701-14), armies of Louis XIV once again laid waste to the Palatinate. In 1707, Marshal Villars and his pillaging horde duplicated the destruction and cruelties of the previous visits by the French to the Rhine Valley. The capital city of Heidelberg was severely damaged as were the sacred tombs of the German emperors at Worms. The vindictive French monarch boasted that "a crow flying over would starve" so complete was the devastation.

THE EXODUS

By the end of the year 1708, it was abundantly clear to the suffering people of the Palatinate that there was little hope for peace and prosperity in their homeland. Continuous warfare, the clash of religious creeds, the collapse of their agricultural base, and the exorbitant tribute they were forced to pay the French convinced many that there was no prospect of rearing their families under decent living conditions in the Rhine Valley they cherished.

The critical situation was discussed quietly in family and small neighborhood gatherings during the severe winter months of 1708-09. People were fearful of news of any mass migration reaching the ears of the Elector of Palatine, who naturally would oppose any such loss of citizenry.

A Lutheran clergyman, Rev. Joshua Kocherthal, had made a trip to England in 1706 to familiarize himself with the English colonies in America. Upon his return to the Palatinate, he wrote a pamphlet filled with glowing descriptions of the settlement opportunities in America.

In addition, William Penn of England had made two trips through the Palatinate to try to encourage migration to his newly acquired province of Pennsylvania. Penn was the author of a law naturalizing foreign Protestants which allowed them to purchase land and engage in trade. This in itself was a great incentive for emigration from the Palatinate to England. Other English-American agents of colonial landlords were also active in soliciting immigrants for their own overseas plantations in America. Labor in the colonies at this time was very scarce and costly.

During the severe winter of 1708-09 thousands perished from lack of shelter, clothing, and food. The weather was so horrendous that all the rivers of northern Europe were ice-bound until late February and the fruit trees and grapevines were decimated.

In 1708, the Reverend Kocherthal and a small group of Palatines visited England and petitioned Queen Anne for help for their settlement in America. Queen Anne's heart ached for the plight of the "poor Palatines,"[2] influenced in part by the fact that her consort, Prince George of Denmark, was himself a Reform Lutheran.

The petition was granted by the London Board of Trade, who decided that these Palatines might be useful "in the production of naval stores and as a protection against the French and their Indians." Queen Anne issued "an order for clothing, tools and to make the Palatines denizens of the Kingdom without charge."[3]

The Board of Trade further recommended that the incoming Governor Lovelace grant the Reverend Kocherthal land for a glebe and that twenty pounds be allowed for clothes and books. This group of fifty-five Palatines sailed with Governor Lovelace for New York in October 1708, on the ship *Globe*, arriving in the city after a nine weeks' voyage.

THE MIGRATION TO AMERICA

At the very end of the year 1708, this group of pioneer Palatines landed at the mouth of Quassaick Creek near present day Newburgh, sixty miles north of New York City, where they founded the first Palatine settlement in the province of New York and quickly built crude log cabins. Governor Lovelace allotted the Reverend Kocherthal five hundred acres of land for church purposes, two hundred additional acres for Kocherthal's family and fifty acres to each of the other people in the small party.

Lovelace took good care of this initial group of Palatines at Newburgh, providing an allowance of nine pence per day, food, and other essentials. No covenant or contract was ever signed by these settlers. Then, unfortunately for the little colony, Governor Lovelace, their guardian angel, passed away on May 6, 1709 from an illness he had contracted on the voyage over.

In August of 1709, the Reverend Kocherthal sailed back to England to lay the conditions of the fledgling colony before Queen Anne and the London Board of Trade. It was his hope that he could secure a permanent provision for the financial support of his compatriots.

He was astounded to find that thousands of Palatines had, in the meantime, emigrated to England. They were quartered in pitiful conditions in hundreds of tents at Blackheath on the south bank of the Thames River near London or crammed into vacant drafty warehouses and barns.

It is estimated that by the mid-summer of 1709, over thirteen thousand had reached London. Many had fled the Palatinate in small open boats via the Rhine River, taking four weeks to reach Rotterdam, Holland. Often they were delayed by the demands for river tolls, but the sympathetic Burgemeester of Rotterdam appropriated seven hundred fifty guilders and solicited private charity for the flood of refugees. In England, both the Whig Party and the Church of England established funds for the relief of the Palatines.

The exodus from the German state became more perilous when the Elector of Palatine issued an edict forbidding any more of his subjects to leave his principality. After this ruling many were forced to seek an overland route to Holland. Food, money, and clothing were generously provided along the way by fellow countrymen.

The British authorities became alarmed because of the immense expense of providing for the vast deluge of immigrants and tried to stop the rush to England. Though Holland also tried to stem the tide of refugees, they still kept arriving.

Then came a turn in the tide of English public sympathy. The great number of refugees and how to deal with them had become quite bothersome to the British government. The Tory Party in Parliament opposed the voting of funds for the relief of the Palatines and, as a result, they became a political *cause célèbre*. The overall crowded conditions of their crude sheltering had made many of them ill, and sickness ran rampant. English labor officials complained that wages in areas where the immigrants were housed had dropped considerably.

The Palatines had expected quick transportation to the American colonies, but instead were mired in months of delay while the London Board of Trade pondered plans for their future. It is estimated that almost one thousand men, women, and children died from disease while British authorities dallied.

Finally on August 30, 1709, the London Board of Trade began to consider a plan to relocate the remaining Palatines in London to the province of New York. It was suggested to Her Majesty to relocate them to land along the Schoharie Creek and Mohawk River that was best suited to produce goods from enormous American resources such as pitch, tar, rosin, hemp, and timber. These goods could be used to supply British naval storehouses. It was also suggested that these Palatines could provide a valuable service as a security buffer against French and Indian aggressors originating in Canada.

As mentioned earlier, four Iroquois "kings," including Hendrick, would visit London in April of 1710, in the company of Peter and John Schuyler as guests of Queen Anne. The "kings" were introduced to Her Majesty with great pomp and ceremony. Gifts were exchanged, including wampum. During their tour of England, the Iroquois leaders were exposed to the horrible living conditions of the Palatine refugees. One of the chiefs made an unsolicited gift to the queen of a tract of his land along Schoharie Creek for the use and benefit of the distressed Germans.

In October of 1709, Col. Robert Hunter received his commission and instructions as the new royal governor of the colony of New York. As a major, Hunter had been wounded at Marlborough's epic victory at Blenheim and had sailed for America as lieutenant governor of Virginia, but was made a captive of French privateers until he was exchanged in the Spring of 1708. In November of 1709, Hunter presented to the Crown an elaborate plan for the settlement of Palatines in New York. The covenant called for the granting of land and goods to the settlers in exchange for services rendered. In essence, it was a condition of indentured servitude of undefined length.

And so under the iron grip of the London Covenant of 1709, three thousand Palatines sailed on April 10, 1710 with their royal governor in ten ships stocked with "600 tents and 600 firelocks with bayonets and ammunition".[4] The overcrowded conditions, foul air, vermin, poor food, and drinking water caused many on board to fall ill. Over four hundred refugees were buried at sea and, later, over two hundred more in the fertile soil of the brave new world they never lived to experience.

The survivors, who had faced the desolation of war, felt the pangs of hunger and the loss of loved ones, resolutely stepped off the plank of the first ship to arrive in New York harbor on June 13, 1710, prepared to face new trials in the frontier wilderness. The records show that about half of the Palatine men were farmers. The other half were carpenters, blacksmiths, schoolmasters, weavers, brick-makers, bakers, millers, masons, coopers, tailors, vinedressers, herdsmen, shoemakers, butchers, brewers, tanners, wheelwrights, stonecutters, silversmiths, saddlers, locksmiths, joiners, bookbinders, tilemakers, surgeons, hatters, and gardeners.

One of the first challenges they faced came in the personage of Robert Livingston, who has been labeled as one of the most unscrupulous land speculators in early New York history. It has been alleged that Livingston was a silent partner of the infamous pirate, Captain William Kidd. Governor Hunter purchased six thousand acres from Livingston on behalf of the Palatines on the east side of the Hudson River in the vicinity of Columbia and Dutchess Counties.

There was some question as to the legality of the Livingston Grant, however, Hunter immediately silenced the critics by having the colonial council issue a new confirmatory grant which also gave Livingston a seat on the New York Provincial Assembly. Livingston was also given the contract for supplying the Palatines with all of the necessities of life. The bills handed to the British government were enormous; in two years they amounted to 76,000 pounds sterling. It is unlikely that much of this windfall directly benefited the settlers. Most of the equipment and supplies promised by Livingston had not been delivered to the Palatines by midsummer 1711.

Each of the Palatine settlers was given seven acres of land on the east bank of the Hudson River at Livingston Manor. This was far short of the forty acres promised in the London Covenant. The assignment of such a small plot of land to each family seemed an insult to these men who had been among the best farmers in Europe. The English were more interested in the settlers' ability to produce tar and pitch for the British navy. By November of 1711, there were 2,200 Palatines engaged in the naval stores project. In exchange for their services, the English authorities also provided the Palatines with beef purchased in New York City; the portions doled out were small and the quality was poor.

In 1711, three hundred Palatines also participated in a failed British military expedition to Canada. Support promised by the English navy never materialized and the foot column marched back home without any positive results to show for their efforts.

During the hard winter of 1712-13, the distress of the Palatines became unbearable. Both food and clothing were scarce. The starving settlers became determined to rid themselves of the selfish supervision of Robert Livingston. Recalling the Iroquois king's gift of land in the valley of the Schoharie to the British queen, many Palatines decided to emigrate to that region.

They started the journey to the Schoharie Valley in March 1713. No roads existed and deep snow covered the ground as they trod forward, cold, hungry, and exhausted. Refugees once again, they had neither wagons nor animals for the transportation of the sick, aged, or young. All belongings had to be carried on their backs and there was little to eat. If it wasn't for the assistance of sympathetic neighboring Indians, many would have starved or frozen to death.

Few settlements had as difficult a beginning as those in the Schoharie Valley. Rough logs furnished the material for huts, clothes were made mostly from skins of wild animals. As no one possessed a plow, the settlers were forced to dig furrows into the ground with their knives. As they had no mill, the first harvest was crushed between stones. Initially, it was almost a biblical existence, and the Palatines compared their treatment by the English authorities as the Pharaoh to the Israelites.

After toiling for two years and by the sweat of their own brows, conditions steadily improved and the Palatines finally saw reason to be optimistic about their future in the colony of New York. Then came the news that Governor Hunter had sold the very lands in the Schoharie Valley the Palatines had so diligently improved to land speculators, including Robert Livingston. Governor Hunter hoped that by the sale of these lands he could force the Palatines back into the Hudson River camps or out to a more exposed sector of the New York frontier. The Palatines were given two unfair options—repurchase the land at exorbitant prices or evacuate the premises.

A principal leader of the Schoharie Palatines at this time was John Conrad Weiser. Hunter learned that Weiser planned to go to England to plead the case of the settlers. The governor did not want the controversy publicly aired in Great Britain and so sent Deputy Sheriff Adams to arrest Weiser. When the sheriff arrived at Weiserdorf, the men were at work in the fields and woodlands. But when the women learned of his mission, they pulled Adams from his horse and dragged him through pools where the pigs wallowed, rode him on a rail, broke two of his ribs, and left him half dead on a bridge on the road leading to Albany, where he was later rescued. This temporarily staved off any further interference from the royal authorities. The settlers continued to plow and work the land, providing for their families. In 1718, John Conrad Weiser sailed for England to plead the case of the Palatines in the matter of the Schoharie land title controversy before the Crown. At the same time, Governor Hunter was traveling to the identical destination in a quest to have his debts reimbursed for the failed naval stores project.

When Hunter learned of the presence of the Palatine delegation, he doggedly opposed them at every step. The Palatines' good friend Queen Anne had died and a new cabinet controlled British policy. Weiser carried his case to the highest British court, the Lord Justices' Court. His plea for fairness was rejected and he returned to his Schoharie Valley home in 1723 a disappointed man.

SETTLING IN THE MOHAWK VALLEY

Hunter resigned his post while in England in 1720 and William Burnett was appointed to succeed him. When the new royal governor arrived in the province, he was immediately contacted by Palatine leaders about lands for settlement in the Mohawk Valley. In 1721, Governor Burnett allowed several families to purchase land from the Mohawk Indians and, in 1722, about sixty families were given permission to begin the migration from the Hudson and Schoharie Valleys to the banks of the mighty Mohawk River. The Stone Arabia Patent, deeded in 1723, and the German Flatts Patent, deeded in 1725, resulted from this last exodus of the Palatines who had begun under such severe hardship in the devastated Rhine Valley fifteen years before.

One of the Palatine families moving to the Mohawk Valley from Scoharie Creek at this time was Johan Jost Herkimer, his wife Catherine, and their eldest daughter Magdalena. Folklore tells us that Johan Jost paddled about in a canoe along the Mohawk River looking for a suitable place to settle and at a bad rift in the river channel he went ashore. He came across some Mohawk Indians and asked them permission to build a cabin; they refused. Then Johan Jost noticed that a group of the Mohawks were struggling to carry a very heavy canoe to the river. Johan Jost motioned to the braves to pick up one end of the canoe as he lifted the other end by himself. Together they transported it to the water's edge. The Mohawks, admiring the strong Herkimer, clapped him on the back and called him "Kouari" (the bear). They then granted him permission to build the cabin.

Johan Jost became a successful farmer and also exchanged rum and hardware for beaver with Indian and white trappers. Tall and powerfully built, he amazed the local Mohawks and Oneidas with his feats of strength. Besides speaking his native German tongue, he spoke English and Indian dialects, becoming a valuable interpreter for all parties. Next to Sir William Johnson, he became the most powerful and respected man in the valley. In 1728, Johan Jost and Catherine's first son, Nicholas, was born. Forty-nine years hence, as commander of the Tryon County Militia Brigade, he would lead eight hundred of his valley neighbors into the bloody ravine at Oriskany.

In the decades prior to the French and Indian War, other settler families would also gain prominence in the Mohawk Valley. Besides Herkimer, they included Klock, Fox, Helmer, Timmerman, Demuth, Walrath, Van Slyck, Bellinger, Petri, Smith, Staring, and Weaver to name only a few. Over a period of fifty years, they carved out several settlements in the frontier wilderness including the aforementioned Stone Arabia and German Flatts, Palatine Bridge, Herkimer and Fort Herkimer, Fort Klock and the present sites of Fort Plain, St. Johnsville, Little Falls, Mohawk, Ilion, and Frankfort. The towns of Fonda, Canajoharie, Johnstown, and Cherry Valley also sprang up in this era.

Of course, the Palatines were not the only ethnic group in the valley. Scotch and Irish settlers, encouraged by the presence of Sir William Johnson, also came to the Mohawk Valley. In some cases, whole Scottish clans emigrated from the Highlands intact with their own tribal chieftains. Sir William Johnson's Irish of County Meath were sprinkled around his settlement. Pioneers of Dutch extraction, holdovers from their nation's period of glory in the former colony of New Netherland, also remained.

DOMESTIC LIFE

The daily existence of the settlers was fraught with backbreaking labor from dawn to dusk. First a patch of the forest would have to be cleared to build a log cabin and plant crops. Fences were built and crude roads were constructed between homesteads. Eventually, life would become more comfortable with the erection of a large two-story home made of planks, bricks, or stones. Some of the more enterprising settlers would expand their holdings to include a saw or grist mill. Barns would be constructed to house the livestock. From these humble beginnings, settlements would blossom in the wilderness.

Everyone worked around the pioneer home—man, woman, and child. Settler families were generally large in size, in part due to the enormous workload necessary to survive and prosper. There were berries to pick, chickens and ducks to look after, water to fetch, cows to milk, clothes to wash, fields to tend, crops to harvest, wild game to hunt, candles and soap to make, and wool to dye and to weave on the loom into cloth for clothing and blankets.

Neighbors were always ready to assist with difficult tasks. Major jobs that would take a single family months to complete, were accomplished in a matter of days by group working sessions called "bees." The various activities included barn-raising, logging, fencing, apple picking, threshing, spinning and quilting bees to name just a few.

Sunday worship was also an essential element of colonial life. One of the first structures built in a settlement would be a church. The Old Palatine Church, founded in 1749, and the Stone Arabia Reformed Church, founded in 1725, are surviving examples of these institutions.

During the course of the Palatine immigrants' terrible sea voyage to

America in 1710, seventy-four children had become orphans. After their arrival, Governor Hunter apprenticed several of them out to New York City merchants and tradespeople. This caused bitter resentment among the Palatines against the governor and would later be listed as one of their grievances in their petition to the Lord Justices Court.

PETER ZENGER

One of these orphaned apprentices was John Peter Zenger. His employer was New York's first printer, William Bradford, who was a kind gentlemen who gave young John Peter a good home and education. Zenger would open the second newspaper and publishing business in the colony of New York. He became a fearless champion of freedom. This is an extract from his *Weekly Journal* in 1734: "We see men's deeds destroyed, judges arbitrarily replaced, new courts erected without the consent of the legislature, by which it seems to me trials by jury are taken away when the governor pleases; men of known estates denied their votes contrary to the recent practices of the best exposition of any law."[5]

The colonists were stirred by such plain speaking, but it raised the ire of Gov. William Cosby, who had Zenger arrested for libel and was denied bail. The distinguished elderly Scottish attorney, Andrew Hamilton, was brought from Philadelphia to defend him.

After languishing nearly a year in jail, Zenger was brought to trial before Judge DeLancey, and in spite of the court's vehement charge to the contrary, he was acquitted by the jury. In his summation, Hamilton had declared: "The question before the court, and you gentlemen of the jury, is not of small nor private concern, it is not the cause of a poor printer, nor of New York alone, which you are trying! No! It may in its consequences affect every free man that lives under a British government on the Main of America!"[6]

These were prophetic words which would foreshadow the later sentiments of Thomas Paine in his treatise, "Common Sense," and the spirit of 1776. The night after the acquittal of John Peter Zenger, New York engaged in a wild demonstration of joy. The Palatine orphan had become the founding father of freedom of the press in America.

THE FRENCH AND INDIAN WAR

Approximately twenty-five years of peace and prosperity were brought to an abrupt halt in the Mohawk Valley with the commencement of the French and Indian War. The first blow in the valley would be struck by a French and Indian expedition led by Lt. Gaspard Joseph Chaussegros de Lery against the Oneida Carry and the tiny garrison at Fort Bull. At this military outpost, the storehouse of which had been built by Capt. Marcus Petri of German Flatts, de Lery and his command of three hundred and sixty men, including troops of Les Compagnies de la Marine, Canadian bush fighters and Indian allies, attacked on March 27, 1756.

Shielded by scattered trees and clusters of fringe growth, they snuck up along the creek bed to within a few hundred feet of the fort. Along the beach de Lery could see men busy loading bateaux. Suddenly, in disregard to the lieutenant's order for stealth, the Indians let out a shrill war cry, and de Lery had no choice but to order a charge at the double quick toward the fort with bayonets leveled. Meanwhile, seeing their safe passage to the fort blocked, the men at the bateaux scattered into the woods.

The French and Indians pressed the muzzles of their muskets into the narrow openings in the stockade posts and blasted volley after volley of deadly fire into the little cluster of determined defenders. De Lery's men chopped furiously at the fort's gate with their axes, while he repeatedly called upon garrison commander, Lieutenant Bull, to surrender. Each time de Lery received a response of musket fire.

Finally, the heavy gate crashed in and the French swarmed into the compound, butchering all around them. Lieutenant Bull fell defending the gate. His wife remained in her husband's quarters hoping to escape, but a Canadian irregular entered the room and grabbed her by the waistbelt. Mrs. Bull screamed and slapped his face. In a rage, he lunged at her with his bayonet and pierced her throat. She fell, gurgling in blood, to the floor.

The French soldiers looted what they could find and then broke into the powder magazines and set them ablaze. De Lery and this troops hurried from the fort as it disintegrated into an inferno. An Indian scout warned the lieutenant that a large sortie from nearby Fort Williams was on the way.

Withdrawing from the area, de Lery and his men began the long trek back to Canada. Accompanying them were the handful of prisoners from Fort Bull who had miraculously managed to escape death during the frenzied massacre, including William Campbell, an interpreter and trader from German Flatts. Several days later, William Johnson would view the carnage at Fort Bull and remark "all were inhumanly butchered and all scalped."[7]

In November of 1757, the ruthless French and their native allies returned to wreak more havoc in the Mohawk Valley. French general de Belletre attacked the German Flatts settlement of Palatine's Village north of the Mohawk River on November 12, burned sixty houses and many other structures, killed forty settlers, and took another one hundred fifty captive. Though warned by Oneida scouts, the villagers scoffed at the news and made no preparations for the invasion. Many people escaped over the ford in the Mohawk River to Fort Herkimer where they took refuge. The garrison of two hundred fifty soldiers at the fort watched and did nothing as the massacre evolved and the settlement burned.

An enemy raiding party attacked the southside settlements on April 30, 1758, killing thirty of the inhabitants and destroying some property. This time the young commandant of the troops at nearby Fort Herkimer responded differently. He was Captain Nicholas Herkimer, newly commissioned in the militia by Governor DeLancey on January 5. At the first sign of danger, Herkimer collected, within the stockade, all the inhabitants of the surrounding settlements he could gather before an attack was launched. The courageous captain then led out a detachment of rangers who met the enemy and drove them into the woods after killing or wounding fifteen of their number. The battered French raiders hightailed it back north.

The year 1760 proved to be an eventful year in the Mohawk Valley. Lord Amherst's army of ten thousand British and colonial militia troops passed through en route to his conquest of Canada. He observed all of the recent forts built to guard the territory along his line of march near the Mohawk River, including Forts Johnson, Canajoharie, Klock, Hendrick, Herkimer, Schuyler, and Stanwix. Fort Stanwix in particular would play an important role in the revolutionary drama which would unfold in the valley in 1777.

Also in 1760, Johannes Roof founded the first white settlement within the borders of present-day Oneida County near Fort Stanwix. Later in that same year, Palatine prisoners taken during the earlier French raids in the valley were repatriated home after the fall of Quebec.

On October 26, 1760, a new king ascended to the throne of England, George III, who would later chide his colonial subjects in America for formulating a desperate conspiracy.

A PERIOD OF GROWTH

The decade prior to the onset of the American War of Independence was characterized by another period of growth and development in the Mohawk Valley. It is estimated that by 1771 the white population in the valley was approaching fourteen thousand.

Nicholas Herkimer built his new estate, in 1764, near the present city of Little Falls on the south bank of the Mohawk River. A fine brick house was built on five hundred acres of land given to him by his father. Barns and slave quarters were built to the south of the main structure. Herkimer, as did many of the landed gentry, "employed" a score of African-American slaves. The house is today maintained as a State Historic Site.

In 1765, the Reverend Samuel Kirkland journeyed through the valley on his way to minister his missionary work to the Seneca Nation. However, his life was threatened and he returned to Oneida Castle in 1766 to share his spiritual message with the Oneidas, a calling he performed until his death in 1808. Kirkland's influence on the Oneidas would figure prominently in their decision to side with the patriots in the American Revolution. In 1793, he founded Hamilton Academy in Clinton, New York for the education of the Oneida Indian youths and white children of the surrounding area. This school became Hamilton College in 1812 and remains one of the most prestigious private post-secondary institutions in the United States.

In 1766, Sir William Johnson built Guy Park for his daughter, Mary, and her husband, Col. Guy Johnson, in present day-Amsterdam, New York. This building and grounds are also under the care of the NYS Office of Parks, Recreation, and Historic Preservation. The same year, Jelles Fonda, ancestor of Henry, Jane, and Peter of twentieth century stage and screen fame, erected a sturdy brick house in the settlement of Schenk's Hollow.

On June 1, 1770, Sir William Johnson presented to the Mohawk Nation the Indian Castle Church that he had Col. Samuel Clyde build just west of Fort Plain. Inside was the typical high pulpit of the period; a bell hanging in the white steeple summoned parishioners to worship. Today it remains as the sole representative structure associated with the eighteenth century Indian culture, and the only surviving colonial building on any of the Iroquois castles. The land was donated by Joseph Brant, who had a home there. With the assistance of the Reverend John Stuart, chaplain of Fort Hunter, Brant was actively engaged as a tutor and interpreter. He and Stuart went together to Indian Castle to baptize the children, preach, and administer communion. Brant was also feverishly at work translating and printing a book of common prayer in the Mohawk language.

In 1767, Palatine valley settlers constructed the Fort Herkimer Reformed Dutch Church. The church was stockaded in 1776 and became the famous Fort Herkimer of the Revolution. The chief inspiration behind the building of this place of worship was Nicholas Herkimer's father, Johan Jost Herkimer. In 1770, the building of the Palatine Lutheran Church located on the bypass of State Route 5, between Nelliston and St. Johnsville, was completed. Its twentieth century restoration was made possible by descendants of the original settlers and is today recognized as the cradle of Lutheranism in the Mohawk Valley.

For six days in March of 1768, Sir William Johnson held a council at Johnson Hall with sachems of the Six Nations. The Indians were incensed with the murdering of their people by frontiersmen on the western border and their settlement on lands belonging to the Iroquois. The Senecas threatened war.

The Six Nations had offered to sell their western lands at a similar council in 1765, and the English government was now determined to set a boundary between the Confederacy and the British colonies. This council of 1768 had been held outdoors in the raw March weather, and Sir William became violently ill and was confined to his room for several weeks. This was the beginning of a serious decline in his health which continued until his death six years later.

THE TREATY OF 1768

The council of the Six Nations reconvened at Fort Stanwix on October 24 of the same year. Sir William was accompanied by his sons-in-law, Col. Guy Johnson and Col. Daniel Claus, and twenty large bateaux brimming with gifts for the Native Americans. By this date over three thousand Indians had also reached Fort Stanwix to begin one of the most important council sessions ever held in North America.

On November 5, Sir William Johnson took deed to all the lands of the Six Nations south of the settled boundary line and paid the Iroquois just $10,000 for their interests. The boundary, as adjusted, ran from the mouth of the Tennessee River, followed the Ohio and Allegheny Rivers to Kittaniny, to the west branch of the Susquehanna, and then continued northeastward to the junction, near Oneida Lake, of Canada and Wood Creeks in the north. The land of the Six Nations lay to the north of this boundary. South of it, the Confederacy ceded their interests to the Crown. In one sweeping gesture the representatives of the Six Nations had bartered away their people's ancient birthright.

The boundary line passed through Oneida County, New York in a generally northern direction. You can locate it today by a stone marker on College Hill Road near Route 233, Town of Kirkland.

As the Indians disliked British military outposts in their territory, and because of economic considerations, Fort Stanwix was shut down. The next time it would be occupied by uniformed soldiers it would be the year 1776, and the troops would be rebels to the Crown.

THE FORMATION OF TRYON COUNTY

The year 1772 marked the beginning of a great new county for the Mohawk Valley. It was named Tryon after the current royal governor of the colony of New York. Tryon County was divided into the five districts of Mohawk, Palatine, Canajoharie, German Flatts, and Kingsland. In the same year, the Tryon County Courthouse and Jail were erected at Johnstown, the county seat. The cornerstone was laid on June 26, 1772, in the presence of Sir William Johnson, Governor Tryon, and a crowd of spectators including English, Scottish, Irish, Dutch, Palatine, and Mohawks—a representative ethnic melting pot of the valley.

An attendee recalled "The attendance of British officers and soldiers gave dignity and brilliancy to the event, while over all the group, asserting the power of the Crown, waved the broad folds of the British flag." Surely some of the spectators, soon to be engaged in a bloody struggle with their neighbors in the valley, must have sensed the oppression this flag symbolized. In the frigid dark December of 1772, many settlers in the Mohawk Valley were forced, by the Tory aristocracy, to sign a religious oath of allegiance, swearing loyalty to George III and Protestantism, partly as a guard against Stuart pretensions, but clearly also designed to stem the rising tide of Whig sympathies in the valley. The Tories were worried about the Whig tendency to support libertarian reform perceived by them as a threat to Crown interests.

The powerful Sir William Johnson died on July 11, 1774. Six short weeks after his death, the first meeting of the Palatine District Committee of Safety was held at the tavern of Adam Loucks in Stone Arabia. The attendees would speak of constitutional rights and liberties.

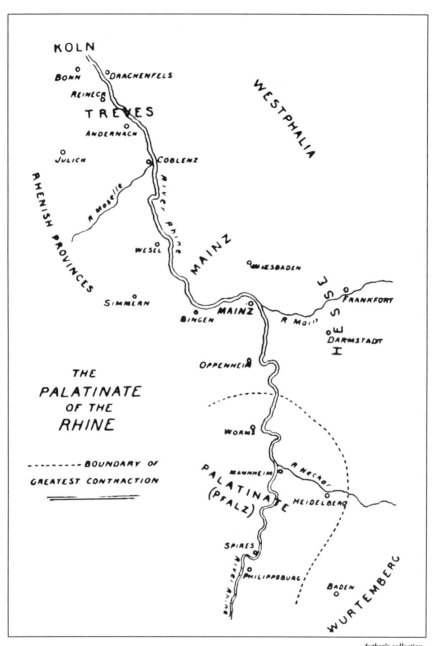

KOLN
BONN
DRACHENFELS
REINECK
TREVES
ANDERNACH
JULICH
COBLENZ
WESTPHALIA
R. Moselle
River Rhine
WESEL
MAINZ
WIESBADEN
SIMMERN
BINGEN
MAINZ
R. Main
FRANKFORT
HESSE
DARMSTADT
THE
PALATINATE
OF THE
RHINE
OPPENHEIM
------- BOUNDARY OF
GREATEST CONTRACTION
WORMS
PALATINATE
(PFALZ)
MANNHEIM
R. Neckar
HEIDELBERG
RHENISH PROVINCES
SPIRES
PHILIPPSBURG
BADEN
WURTEMBERG

The Palatinate, from The Palatine Society's *The Palatines of New York State*

King Louis XIV

The American woodsman, from Lee's *Pictorial History of the American Revolution*, collection of the Oneida County Historical Society

Fleeing the ravages of war, from Lee's *Pictorial History of the American Revolution*, collection of the Oneida County Historical Society

John Conrad Weiser, from The Palatine Society's *The Palatines of New York State*

Flag found in Old Palatine Church, from Palatine Society's *The Palatines of New York State*

Photo by the author

Domestic life in the eighteenth century, courtesy of the National Park Service, Fort Stanwix National Monument

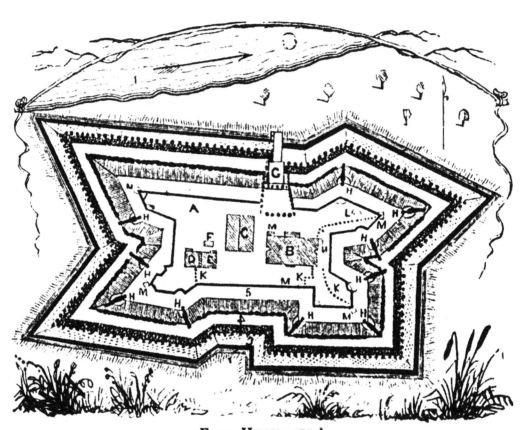

FORT HERKIMER.[1]

Fort Herkimer in 1758, from Greene's *The Mohawk Valley*

Fort Herkimer Church, from Cowen's *The Herkimers and* Schuylers, collection of the Oneida County Historical Society

Photo by the author

Herkimer Home, courtesy of New York State Office of Parks, Recreation, and Historic Preservation, Herkimer Home State Historic Site

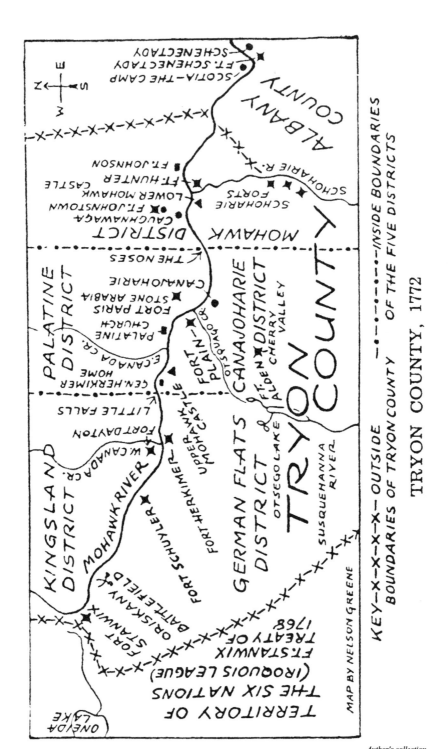

Tryon County in 1772, from Greene's *The Mohawk Valley*

The tree of liberty grows only when
watered by the blood of tyrants
—*Bertrand Barere*

Chapter Five

REVOLUTION

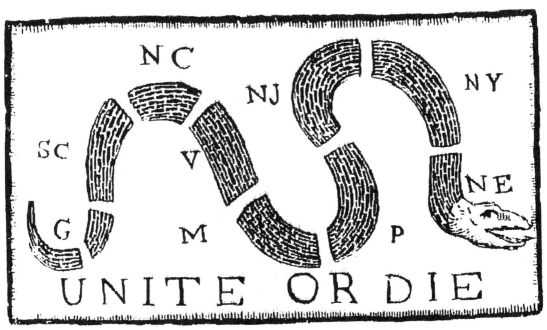

Illustration by Benjamin Franklin to promote unity in the colonies

ROAD TO REVOLUTION

When George III ascended the throne of Great Britain in 1760, England was a nation intoxicated with victory. Day after day the London church bells pealed loudly to declare yet another triumph on the field of battle against France. The British *Annual Register* for 1759 noted, "In no one year since she was a nation has she been favored with so many successes, both by sea and by land, and in every quarter of the globe."[1] Trade and manufacturing were at an all time high.

Yet, by the time the Treaty of Paris was signed in 1763, the English people were weary of constant war, and anxious to see high taxation returned to lower peacetime levels. Key questions remained for the Crown to resolve. Who would administer the burgeoning American empire? Who would pay the war debts? Military victory had brought a new set of issues.

The popular image of a revolution as a powder keg lit by a single spark is a distorted one. A revolution is more like a pot of oozing liquid—heated and left unattended it simmers and seethes until the pot boils over. This was the case with the American Revolution. A law of physics states that for every action there is a reaction. Human nature is not dissimilar. For every act imposed by the British Parliament upon the people of the thirteen colonies from the years 1759 through 1774, there was a reaction. Verbal protest gave way to defiance and defiance led to open rebellion.

Oppressive measures began in 1759 with Parliament's disallowance of policies passed by the popular assemblies in the colonies. The enacting of the Writs of Assistance empowered royal customs officials to break into homes and stores and to dictate judicial tenure in colonial courts.

The Proclamation of 1763 forbade western settlement beyond the Appalachian Divide, eliminated provincial paper currency as legal tender, and bolstered the authority of the customs department and vice-admiralty courts in relation to the enforcement of the Navigation Acts.

In 1763, Lord George Grenville had become the king's chief minister. He pushed through Parliament a series of controversial bills including the Sugar Act of 1764, imposing a tax on imported molasses, and the Stamp Act of 1765, which mandated that an official stamp be affixed to all wills, titles, and other legal documents as well as on dice and playing cards. The pot was beginning to boil over.

The reaction of the colonists to such measures was swift and boisterous. A Boston town meeting denounced "taxation without representation." Then in 1765, the Quartering Act was passed requiring the colonies to provide barracks and supplies for the British troops stationed in America. The pot seethed more furiously.

The British government was dumbfounded by the intense opposition to these additional "revenue enhancements," for they were earmarked for the defense of the colonies. The colonists, however, no longer considered the French or Indians a serious threat to their domestic security. They considered the Quartering Act unnecessary.

The fires of protest leapt higher. In the Virginia Assembly, a newly elected, tall, red-headed, rather shabbily dressed twenty-nine-year-old member introduced resolutions asserting that no one but the assembly had the right to impose taxes upon the colony. Patrick Henry accented his remarks by exclaiming, "If this be treason, make the most of it!"[2]

Following Virginia's lead, in October 1765 delegates from nine colonies met in New York for a Stamp Act Congress. They petitioned the Crown against taxation without their consent and then urged the colonies to boycott British goods. Groups of men were organized in each colony to make sure the Stamp Act was not obeyed. They called themselves the Sons of Liberty. Tax collectors were pressured, with threats of violence, to resign their posts. In Boston, the Sons of Liberty forced their way into Lieutenant Governor Thomas Hutchinson's mansion, vandalized it and burned his papers. Hutchinson lamented, "The hellish crew fell upon my house with the rage of devils."[3]

North of New York City lay great blocks of land acquired by patronage and fraud. The previously cited Robert Livingston family was one such example. They succeeded in expanding a grant of a few thousand acres into holdings of 160,000 acres by falsifying maps when the boundaries were drawn. Knowing how the land had been illegally garnered, some tenants claimed title to the farmlands they worked. They were labeled "Levellers," after the name of a popular party that sprang up during the English Revolution of the 1640's.

The tenants refused to pay their rents and rioted against the sheriff's deputies. By the spring of 1766 the circumstances were so dire that British troops had to be called in. One military officer described the critical situation in his journal: "June 29—Seventeen hundred of the Levellers with firearms are collected at Poughkeepsie. All the jails broke open through all the counties this side of Albany, by people headed by William Pendergrast. Eight thousand cartridges sent up to the 28th Regiment. July 10—This morning arrived the 28th Regiment with Pendergrast, the principal country rebel ringleader. August 19—William Pendergrast found guilty of high treason and received sentence of death, begged leave of the court to deliver a few words, viz: That if opposition to government was deemed rebellion, no member of that court was entitled to set upon his trial."[4]

Staunch resistance to the Stamp Act brought about its repeal. But many unpopular measures remained to nag at the colonists, and new annoyances were added. It should be remembered that at this juncture most people in the colonies still thought of themselves as Englishmen; they were not begging for new liberties or independent nationhood. Instead, they feared the loss of freedoms they had long enjoyed.

In 1767, Parliament passed the Townshend Acts, named after their initiator, the brilliant but reckless king's chief minister whose nickname was "Champagne Charlie."[5] Brushing aside the lessons learned by the Stamp Act, Townshend hastily levied new duties on such everyday items as glass, lead, paint, paper, and tea. Colonial opposition continued to escalate from resistance to revolution. On March 5, 1770, in Boston, a confrontation occurred between an unruly mob and British troops guarding the customhouse. Jeers and snowballs were tossed in the troops' direction. The tension erupted into bloodshed when the soldiers panicked and shots rang out. When the smoke cleared, five Bostonians lay sprawled in the snow, dead.

Parliament reconsidered the Townshend Acts, but not the one on tea. In 1773, the Tea Act was shoved down the throats of the colonists, imposing further duty on the popular beverage. Sam Adams's concept of Committees of Correspondence between towns and colonies was extremely useful as a network, and the boycotting of British tea in protest was quickly arranged. When George Washington celebrated his re-election to the Virginia House of Burgesses, an English visitor made note of the refreshments served: "a hogshead of toddy...coffee and chocolate, but no tea. This herb is in disgrace."[6] In Boston Harbor, three ships docked and refused to depart with their tea. Sam Adams stood up at a town meeting and said in a reluctant tone, "This meeting can do nothing more to save the country."[7] This was a signal, and that evening comrades of the Sons of Liberty, poorly disguised as Mohawks in war paint, dumped 342 chests of fine tea into the harbor.

Recognizing Massachusetts as a hotbed of sedition, the Crown moved to isolate the province from the other colonies by the passage of the "Intolerable Acts" in early 1774. Two elements of these measures were to reorganize the government of Massachusetts to strengthen royal control, and the port of Boston was slammed shut. The Quebec Act extended this province south to the Ohio River. The Americans viewed this as a threat to their western lands. A new Quartering Act was also thrust upon the already resentful colonists.

PALATINE MALCONTENT

The seeds of malcontent were beginning to sprout in the valley of the Mohawk as well. As mentioned earlier, the Tory aristocracy in the Mohawk Valley required the leading citizens of the region to sign a religious oath of allegiance on December 8, 1772. The document was possibly a ruse to get valley Whig leaders to pledge allegiance to George III, a circumstance which later could be interpreted to mean a blanket endorsement of all actions of the Crown. Or the paper may have been used to identify the strongest of the opposition, those declining to sign the document.

The rambling oath read in part:

> "I do sincerely promise and swear that I will be faithful and bear true allegiance to his Majesty King George the Third so help me God.... I do believe in my conscience that not any of the descendants of the person who pretended to be the Prince of Wales during the lifetime of King James the Second and since his decease pretended to be and took upon himself the stile and title of King James the Third of England hath any right or title whatsoever to the Crown of this Realm...."[8]

Considering the horrors of the Palatine's past experience with the Catholic King Louis XIV, it was not difficult for them to reject the Catholic Stuarts and sign an oath of allegiance to the Protestant King George III. And in any case, in 1772, under the firm guiding hand of Sir William Johnson and regardless of disputes over taxation, Whigs and Tories were still loyal to the king and men of both parties willingly signed the document. Within twenty months, this would change dramatically.

The signatories to this document allow us to bring to the stage those gentlemen who would be principal figures in the coming conflict. The Tories are represented by Sir John Johnson, son of Sir William; Colonels Guy Johnson and Daniel Claus; and Colonels John Butler and Hendrick Frey. On November 25, 1772, the first election in the new County of Tryon had been held and Guy Johnson and Hendrick Frey were elected to represent the county in the State Assembly. They would retain close ties with the influential Butler family represented by John and his son Walter, who would play the role of the villain in the upcoming drama which was ready to unfold in the valley.

If Sir John and Col. Guy Johnson, Claus, and Butler did not possess the influence and reputation of Sir William with the Iroquois, they certainly tried to compensate for it with ardor and zeal. Upon his appointment as Superintendent of Indian Affairs, Col. Guy Johnson immediately named Joseph Brant as his secretary. Seeing the coming storm, they tried to prejudice the Six Nations against the Whig cause.

There were times when the Whigs, or future Patriots, by their own actions caused friction with the Iroquois. Consider the case of George

Klock. For years Klock had been illegally homesteading on Indian land and stubbornly refusing to release it.

On July 28, 1772, while visiting Johnson Hall, Joseph Brant outlined the entire Klock controversy to Governor Tryon saying, "We rely on your justice for relief, and hope we may obtain it, so as to continue to live peaceably."[9] A resolution was not forthcoming and, in May of 1774, the Canajoharie Indians forced a meeting with George Klock at his home. About twenty Mohawks were in the group including Joseph Brant and Brant Johnson. The Indians took the law into their own hands and gave Klock a beating. Klock subsequently agreed to sign the release, setting a date of June 25 with the Mohawks for the transferal. When the Indians returned to his home on this date, George Klock was nowhere to be found.

The enraged Mohawks threatened Klock's family and killed some sheep that belonged to his sons. Klock had a brother named Jacob, who would become Colonel of the Palatine Regiment (Second Battalion), Tryon County Militia Brigade, and who would lead them during the Battle of Oriskany.

It was said that two-thirds of the people of the Mohawk Valley during this period were of Whig sentiment and that one-third were Tories. Ironically, then, most of the signers of the oath of allegiance would become rebels against the Crown. Five of them would emerge as primary officers of the Patriot's Tryon County Militia including Nicholas Herkimer, Brigade Commander; Harmanus Van Slyck and John Eisenlord, majors in the Palatine Regiment; Peter Bellinger, Colonel of the German Flatts Regiment; and General Herkimer's brother-in-law, Frederick Visscher, Colonel of the Mohawk Regiment (Third Battalion). Three of these leaders would perish as a result of wounds suffered on that bloody day at Oriskany.

In late August of 1774, twelve prominent men of the Palatine District gathered at Adam Louck's tavern in Stone Arabia for a historic meeting. It was a warm day and the door was thrown wide open. On the wall hung prints of Martin Luther, Frederick the Great, George III, and surprisingly, Louis XIV. The "Sun King" was put in the frame upside down and under it were these lines in German:

> "This is the man we all should hate
> Who drove us from our home
> Who burned the Old Palatinate
> And sent us forth to roam."[10]

Through an open door at one end of the bar another long, low room was in view, and inside two men were busily engaged in writing, while others stood gesturing and speaking in animated conversation.

These were the patriarchs of the Palatine District of the county of

Tryon. They had come together to discuss the growing crisis in the country and to take measures to assert their rights and to protest the growing oppression of the British Parliament. At one end of a long oak table sat Maj. John Frey, busy with a fountain pen and having to endure the suspicious stares of some in the room because his brother, Hendrick, was a noted Tory. At the opposite end of the table sat his brother-in-law, Christopher P. Yates. Yates had come to the district from Schenectady and was a lawyer by profession and considered to be scholarly. Also present was the future Lieutenant Colonel of the Palatine Regiment, Peter Wagner; Jacob Klock, Isaac Paris, Harmanus Van Slyck, Anthony Van Vechten, and Christopher W. Fox, all destined to become officers in the Patriot's Tryon County Militia.

This is a portion of what they boldly wrote on this sweltering day in August 1774:

"Whereas the British parliament has lately passed an act for raising a revenue of our representatives, abridging the privileges of the American Colonies and blocking up the port of Boston; the freeholders and inhabitants of the district of Palatine, of the county of Tryon aforesaid, looking with concern and heartfelt sorrow on these alarming and calamitous conditions, do meet this 27th day of August on this purpose and conclude the resolves following, viz:

I.   That King George the Third is the lawful and rightful lord and sovereign of Great Britain.

II.   With cheerfulness we will always pay submission thereto, as far as we consistently can with the security of the constitutional rights and liberties of English subjects, which are so sacred that we cannot permit the same to be violated.

III.   That we think it is our undeniable privilege to be taxed only with our own consent.

IV.   That the act for blocking up the port of Boston is oppressive and arbitrary...injurious to the inhabitants of Boston, whom we consider as brethren suffering in the common cause.

V.   That we will unite and join with the different districts of this country in anything tending to support and defend our rights and liberties.

VI.   That we think the sending of delegates to a Continental Congress is a salutary measure and absolutely necessary at this alarming crisis."[11]

More meetings in other districts in the region would follow with similar results. The Patriots in the valley of the Mohawk had thrown down the gauntlet and their Loyalist neighbors would obligingly pick it up with resolute vigor.

FIRST CONTINENTAL CONGRESS

The First Continental Congress met on September 5, 1774, in Philadelphia. As the delegates from the thirteen colonies made the journey to this cultured city, they were enthusiastically greeted in each town and hamlet they passed with ringing church bells, firing cannons, and "men, women, and children crowding as if to a coronation." This Congress would forgo the humiliation of further petition to an insensitive and obstinate Parliament and instead appeal directly to the English people. The message implored that the people of Great Britain had "been led to greatness by the hand of liberty; and therefore the people of America, in all confidence, invoked their sense of justice, and prayed for permission to share their freedom."

Fifteen days later the Pennsylvania Assembly entertained the dignitaries of Congress at a dinner in the City Tavern. All in attendance arose in unison when the toastmaster declared, "May the sword of the parent never be stained with the blood of her children."[12] Regrettably, it was a sentiment too late in coming and it fell on deaf ears. The heavy weight of public opinion and official policy on both sides of the Atlantic had been pushed to the edge, and a dramatic encounter on a New England green would soon send it crashing to the depths of bloody rebellion.

At exactly three o'clock on the afternoon of April 18, 1775, an era of troubled peace ended for a whole continent. At that hour patriotic members of the parish of Old North Church in Boston discharged their Loyalist rector and confiscated his keys to the building; within hours these keys were put to good use. Two lanterns were placed in the church steeple as a signal that British troops were moving by water to Concord under the cover of a dark and rainy night. Rumors flew among the colonists that the Redcoats were going to seize the powder ammunition at Concord or, perhaps, were after the Patriot leaders in Lexington. One of the volunteer couriers, Paul Revere, set off on a mad dash to Lexington to warn Sam Adams and John Hancock of the movement.

Lexington armed itself. At dawn on April 19, 1775, Capt. John Parker mustered seventy Minutemen and formed two lines on the common beside the road to Concord. The scarlet column of British soldiers loomed in the distance, led by Maj. John Pitcairn of the Royal Marines. Captain Parker issued his immortal command, "Stand your ground; don't fire unless fired upon; but if they mean to have a war, let it begin here!" A single pistol shot rang out, followed by sputtering volleys. The *Salem Essex Gazette* reported: "Last Wednesday, the troops of his Brittanic Majesty commenced hostilities upon the people of this Province . . . We are involved in all the horrors of a civil war."[13]

REBELLION IN THE VALLEY

In late April, news of Lexington and Concord reached the Mohawk Valley and served to enrage the Loyalists and arouse patriotic sympathies among the Whigs. On May 11, 1775, about three hundred unarmed settlers assembled at the home of John Veeder at Caughnawaga (now Fonda). Their main purposes were to deliberate and also to erect a "Liberty Pole" to show their support for the union of the thirteen embattled American colonies. Among the people gathered there were Sampson Sammons and his three sons, Jacob, Frederick, and Thomas.

Tory officials caught wind of the session and soon Sir John Johnson, accompanied by his two brothers-in-law, Guy Johnson and Daniel Claus, rode to the meeting along with a great number of their Highland retainers armed with swords and pistols. Remaining on his horse, Colonel Guy faced the crowd in front of the Veeder house and began to harangue the crowd backed up by his armed henchmen. "Listen to me you fools! You talk about taking up arms against the king? Do you know the strength of that king? Do you realize that he can put down any insurrection you start?" Jacob Sammons could not resist calling out, "Guy Johnson, you are a liar and a villain!"[14] With a roar, the furious Colonel Guy lunged out and seized Sammons by the throat and struck him with a loaded whip. Jacob delivered a blow which freed him from Johnson's grasp, then flung off his coat preparing to brawl, but two pistols were leveled at his chest. He hesitated and then was knocked down and severely beaten. When he regained consciousness, he slowly rose to his feet and discovered that, except for the Fonda, Visscher, and Veeder families, everyone else had dissipated. This would be only the first of many violent confrontations between Loyalist and Patriot opponents in the valley.

Late in the spring of 1775, Col. Frederick Visscher was parading his regiment of Tryon County Militia at Caughnawaga when Sir John and Lady Johnson rode through the village in their coach. The priggish baronet Johnson alighted and insisted that Visscher dismiss his troops. He and Visscher exchanged words and preceded to scuffle. Johnson threatened to shoot and stab the colonel. Sir John prudently withdrew when one of Visscher's young Irish militiamen retorted: "If ye offer to lift a finger against my master, I'll blow ye through."[15]

In the Mohawk Valley, revolution was very much a personal matter, pitting neighbor against neighbor and blood against blood. It is said that the first shot of the American Revolution west of Albany was fired, in July 1775, by Tory sheriff White at a gang of Whigs who had come to free Jacob Fonda from jail, where he was imprisoned for having strong patriotic sentiments.

On June 2, 1775, the first full meeting of the Tryon County Committee of Safety was held at the house of Warner Tygert, a neighbor and relative of Nicholas Herkimer. On June 11, the committee chose Christopher P. Yates and John Marlett as delegates to the provincial congress. The committee asked Herkimer and Edward Wall to deliver a letter to Guy Johnson protesting his Loyalist leanings. Sir Guy returned a polite but noncommittal reply. The committee now proceeded to take over all of the civic and military functions of the county. Seeing the handwriting on the wall in regards to his future viability, Sir Guy departed for Canada in the company of his family, dependents, and a large number of Mohawk Indians. The next time Colonel Johnson and his native allies would return to the valley it would be as a war party raining terror down upon his former neighbors. Johnson and his large entourage pushed on to Ontario far beyond the reach of the angry valley patriots. From there he went to Montreal, joined by many warriors of the Iroquois Confederacy.

Sir Guy was temporarily out of the picture, but Sir John Johnson remained to play his intrigues in valley affairs in spite of his vow of neutrality. There was ample cause for alarm as the baronet had amassed a large body of well-armed Loyalist followers. In December of 1775, the Continental Congress resolved to send Gen. Philip Schuyler, with two thousand troops, to Tryon County under orders to secure the arms and stores of the Tories and "to apprehend their chiefs."

On January 18, 1776, Schuyler's command met up with Col. Nicholas Herkimer's Tryon County Regiment at Caughnawaga. On this day, a review of the combined body of three thousand soldiers was held on the ice over the Mohawk River. This was the largest American Revolutionary force ever seen in the valley. It was during this review that militiaman Robert Crouse exhibited one of his famed feats of strength. Crouse was a giant of a man and tremendously strong. To the cheering of onlookers, the burly man easily waved the regimental flag with one hand, an accomplishment difficult even for a muscular man using two hands. At the Battle of Oriskany, Robert Crouse would suffer a horrible fate.

On January 20, 1776, Schuyler and Herkimer moved on Johnstown with their massive column. Awed by the overwhelming superiority of the American force, Sir John Johnson and approximately three hundred of his Tory followers surrendered the next day. The proud Highlanders advanced in formation down William Street and ground their arms in front of the Tryon County Courthouse. Sir John was allowed to keep his family coat of arms and placed on his parole of honor. General Schuyler delivered a brief address offering conciliation to the Loyalists. The Tories listened in bitter silence.

Sir John continued his subterfuge from Johnson Hall, supplying Loyalist sympathizers with arms and ammunition through a clandestine route from Canada. Finally, Col. Elisha Dayton was directed to proceed to Johnstown with a portion of Schuyler's regiment and to place the baronet under arrest.

Forewarned by friends in Albany, Sir John fled in the night for Montreal in the company of a large body of retainers and Indian guides. It was a hazardous journey which took nineteen days to complete. The next day Lady Johnson was taken by the Americans to Albany where she was held as a hostage because of her husband's actions.

On August 22, 1776, the following men were named, by majority vote, as field officers for the Patriot's Tryon County Militia:

First Battalion, Canajoharie Regiment
  Nicholas Herkimer, Col.; Ebenezer Cox, Lt. Col.
Second Battalion, Palatine Regiment
  Jacob Klock, Col.; Peter Wagner, Lt. Col.
Third Battalion, Mohawk Regiment
  Frederick Visscher, Col.; Adam Fonda, Lt. Col.
Fourth Battalion, Kingsland and German Flatts Regiment
  Han Yost Herkimer, Col.*; Peter Bellinger, Lt. Col.[16]

*Note: Han Yost Herkimer was Nicholas' brother. Later he would turn Tory and flee to Canada. This defection would damage Nicholas Herkimer's prestige and, as the reader will later learn, have an impact on the debacle at Oriskany. It was not uncommon for valley families to have divided political relations and many families and marriages were shattered by bitter differences. The American War of Independence was in this sense our nation's first civil war.

HERKIMER'S COMMISSION

On September 5, 1776, the Convention of the Representatives of the State of New York commissioned Nicholas Herkimer a Brigadier General to command the Tryon County Militia. His commission reads in part:

IN CONVENTION OF THE REPRESENTATIVES OF THE STATE OF NEW YORK TO NICHOLAS HERKIMER ESQUIRE,

GREETINGS: We reposing especial trust and confidence in

your patriotism valour conduct and fidelity do by these presents constitute and appoint you the said Nicholas Herkimer Brigadier General of the Brigade of Militia of the County of Tryon embodied for the defense of American liberty and for repelling every hostile invasion thereof you are carefully and diligently to discharge the duty of Brigadier General by doing and performing all manner of things thereunto belonging and we do strictly charge and require all officers and privates under your command to be obedient to your orders as Brigadier General and you are to observe and follow such orders and directions from time to time as you shall receive from the present or any future Congress of the United States of America or from this or any future Convention of the Representatives or future Executive Authority of this State or from the Commander in Chief for the time being of the Army of the United States.

Given at Fishkills, the fifth day of September in the year of our Lord one thousand seven hundred and seventy six.[17]

A month before his commission, the forty-eight-year-old Herkimer had married Maria Dygert, a youthful girl of nineteen. She was his second wife, as he had been a widower for several years.

The frontier wilderness which Nicholas Herkimer and the Tryon County Militia were sworn to defend was, perhaps, the most vulnerable to enemy attack of any sector in the thirteen colonies. The English and their Canadian and Indian allies had the potential to launch an attack on the colonies from three directions; from the north from Canada, from the south from New York City, or from the west from Fort Niagara and Oswego.

Four weeks after the Tryon County Militia had been formed, a battalion of Minutemen was organized to serve as scouts or rangers. George Herkimer, brother of Nicholas, was named its colonel and Samuel Campbell served as its lieutenant colonel.

THE CONFEDERACY AFFECTED

The Six Nations of the Iroquois were trapped in the middle of the white man's war. Though they tried to maintain some measure of neutrality, this policy would prove to be a failure. As early as September of 1774, and prior to his hasty, unplanned departure from the Mohawk Valley, Col. Guy Johnson, the newly appointed Superintendent of Indian Affairs, had lobbied the Confederacy hard for their support of the Crown.

At a council to discuss the problem of the western lands, a condolence service was held for Johnson by the sachems to allow him to mourn the death of his great Uncle William. Then according to their ancient custom, they chose a new name for Sir Guy in honor of his new title. Henceforth they would call him "Uraghquadirha," which means "Rays of the Sun Enlightening the Earth." A chief representing each nation repeated the name as Colonel Johnson stood before them. The Iroquois had also brought with them the "Great Old Covenant Chain Belt," a large section of wampum twenty-one rows wide, which signified the chain of friendship between the English and the Six Nations. They reassured Johnson that this sacred trust, the firm link between the two peoples, "which we have kept free from rust, and held fast in our hand. This makes us remember the words that were told to us when it was given, and which we always look upon, if any one offers to disturb that peace and harmony subsisting between us,"[18] was still intact.

Though the Oneidas were influenced by colonial missionary Samuel Kirkland's arguments for the rebel cause, they attempted to remain unbiased. A message from the Oneidas to Governor Trumbull of Connecticut stated: "We are unwilling to join on either side of such a contest, for we love you both—old England and new. Should the great King of England apply to us for our aid—we shall deny him—and should the Colonists apply—we shall refuse."[19]

The Iroquois would be caught up in the conflict, like it or not, because of intense political pressure from both sides and their economic interdependence with the whites. The British insisted upon active support while the rebels requested their neutrality. Though the Iroquois could not afford to be isolationists, they never took up arms against any of the white factions prior to 1777.

—1777—

The year 1777 dawned hazy in the quest for American liberty. Twenty months had passed since the "shot heard 'round the world" at Lexington signaled a call to arms. In the interim, an avalanche of humiliating defeats had been heaped upon the ragged rebel forces, courtesy of the professional armies of His Royal Majesty, George III.

On both Breeds Hill and Bunker Hill, the insurgents held their own in their first major test against the deadly ranks of British bayonets. And Ethan Allen and his Green Mountain Boys and courageous Benedict Arnold were the heroes of the day on May 10, 1775, with their capture of Fort Ticonderoga. However, a host of disasters were to follow.

Launching an aggressive campaign in late fall 1775, the Patriots attempted to create a fourteenth colony through the conquest of Canada. This ill-conceived offensive fizzled out, during a ferocious blizzard, at the gates of the fortress of Quebec on New Year's Eve. Perhaps the greatest loss to the Americans was the death of brave Gen. Richard Montgomery.

On March 17, 1776, the English evacuated Boston. The sizeable garrison and formidable naval flotilla were allowed to withdraw virtually intact. This powerful armada thus remained a threat to the colonists' aspirations of emancipation.

WASHINGTON'S APPOINTMENT

In July of the previous year, the Second Continental Congress had appointed a modest Virginian as general and commander-in-chief of the main American army clustered about Boston. Reluctantly, "Mr. Washington," as the Redcoats called him, had accepted the mantle of leadership and responsibility for those volunteers from New England, New York, New Jersey, Pennsylvania, Maryland, Delaware, and his native Virginia.

Fearing a British seaborne assault on New York City, Washington gradually transferred his troops from New England to Manhattan and Long Island. His combined command of Continentals and militia now numbered almost twenty thousand.

On June 29, 1776, the expected invasion came, competently directed by Gen. William Howe. The American army was split between Long Island and Manhattan and faced the largest expeditionary force ever assembled by the Crown. Washington's ragtag army barely survived a series of running battles at Long Island, Harlem Heights, and White Plains over the next three months. The Americans were pummeled by the crack British regiments and their new allies, soldiers hired by King George III, from the German states, including Hesse-Cassel.

On September 15, Sir William Howe triumphantly occupied New York. Washington's shattered main command, reduced by casualties and desertions to a strength of only six thousand combatants, crossed the Hudson River and retreated through New Jersey. It was perhaps the darkest hour of the American Revolution.

Two events occurred in 1776 that served to bolster the sagging spirits of the Patriots. The first did not take place on a bloody field of glory, but in a private home at Seventh and Market Streets in Philadelphia. There a committee appointed by Congress met to consolidate into proper legal form the various resolutions of the thirteen colonies, thereby defining the nature of the rebellion.

The committee included the aristocratic Thomas Jefferson of Virginia, serene Benjamin Franklin of Pennsylvania, New York's patriarchal Robert Livingston, Connecticut's vocal Roger Sherman, and intellectual John Adams of Massachusetts. It was left to the eloquent writing of Jefferson to interpret their collective thoughts. The final document was presented to the full Congress on an exceptionally humid July day. A resolution was introduced which read in part, "Resolved: that these United Colonies are, and of right out to be, free and independent States; that they are absolved from all allegiance to the British Crown."[20] This was the birth of the Declaration of Independence.

Across the colonies, the declaration was conveyed to assembled troops and townsfolk. Capt. Alexander Graydon, Third Pennsylvania Battalion, summarized the prevailing assessment of the resolution when he said: "The matter is settled now and our salvation depends upon supporting the measure."[21] The reaction of the Sons of Liberty was less staid. They hauled down the gilded statue of King George on the Bowling Green and melted it into bullets for the "Army of Liberty."

The second event transpired in the early hours of December 26, 1776, when General Washington's determined band of citizen-soldiers silently pulled their way across the ice-clogged Delaware River. Their destination was the sleeping town of Trenton, winter headquarters for three Hessian regiments. The groggy Germans were still recuperating from a full day of Christmas "cheer." The element of surprise was complete. In less than one hour, the Americans took over nine hundred prisoners. The news of the stunning victory spread quickly and electrified the Patriots. Miraculously, Washington's beleaguered little army had defeated tough European military professionals.

By 1777, in the northern theater, Brittania ruled the waves and New York; the Patriots controlled Boston and most of the countryside.

King George III and family, from Lee's *Pictorial History of the American Revolution*, collection of the Oneida County Historical Society

Burning of the stamped paper, from Collins' *The Story of America in Pictures*, collection of Fred Reed

The Boston Tea Party, from Collins' *The Story of America in Pictures*, collection of Fred Reed

John Butler, courtesy of
the Niagara Historical Society,
Niagara-on-the-Lake, Ontario

Tories gathered outside the Tryon County Courthouse, from Greene's *The Mohawk Valley*

Delegates to the First Continental Congress, from Collins' *The Story of America in Pictures*, collection of Fred Reed

"First Shots at Lexington" by Alonzo Chappel, from Collins' *The Story of America in Pictures*, collection of Fred Reed

The Tory aristocracy of the Mohawk Valley, from Greene's *The Mohawk Valley*

Philip Schuyler, collection of the Montgomery County Historical Society

"Washington Takes Command," by U.S. Army Corps of Engineers, photographed by author at Fynmore Studio

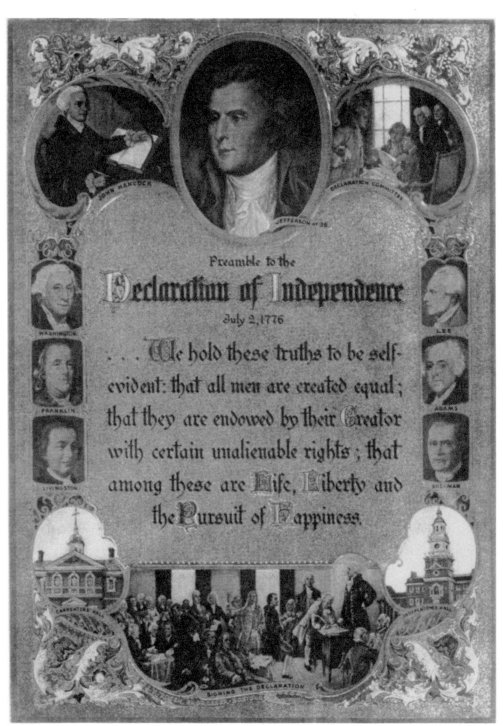

Preamble to the Declaration of Independence

Brig. Gen. Nicholas Herkimer, illustration by David Yahnke

"Infantry of Continental Army," by U.S. Army Quartermaster Department, photographed by author at Fynmore Studio

Strike—till the last armed foe expires;
Strike—for your altars and your fires;
Strike—for the green graves of your sires;
God—and your native land.
                              —*Fitz-Green Halleck*

Chapter Six

THE MARCH

Photo by Patricia Zemken

Marching for the "common good," collection of James Morrison

John Adams characterized 1777 as "The Year of the Hangman" due to the three "7s" in the year which resembled the scaffolding of the hangman's gallows. Washington's Army of Liberty was suffering through a harsh sojourn at its winter quarters in Valley Forge, Pennsylvania. Food, clothing, and other provisions were scarce, and bitter sniping had begun among members of the officer corps. Officers from New York and New England distrusted each other. Empty bellies increased the risk of mutiny and illness among the troops. Guards stood barefoot in the snow. Morale was so low that it was almost as invisible as the thin fabric of the tents covering the shivering men at twilight.

BARON VON STEUBEN

Enter Baron von Steuben, a forty-seven-year-old native of Magdeburg, Germany on the Elbe River. The son of a professional soldier who since infancy had experienced nothing but "guns, drums, trumpets, drills, and parades" in the Prussian tradition established by Friedrich von Grosse (Frederick the Great). At age thirteen he had joined his father as a volunteer during the long and costly siege of Prague. He was a first lieutenant by the time of the Seven Year's War and eventually attained the rank of major on the king's staff. He grew restless in the idle peacetime role of grand marshal in the court of a German prince, and gladly accepted the offer of French war minister Count St. Germain to visit Paris.

When von Steuben arrived, he was surprised to find St. Germain bent over a map of America. A few days later the military veteran stood face to face with Benjamin Franklin. He learned that in exchange for a couple thousand acres of land, the Americans wished to employ the marshal's services in the only field of expertise he knew, military training.

At a subsequent session with St. Germain, the officer agreed to serve the Patriots as an advisor in military matters with the conditional rank of lieutenant general. On September 26, 1777, fifteen days after the Battle of Brandywine, Baron Frederick William Augustus Henry Ferdinand von Steuben embarked for America.

Over the next few years, Baron von Steuben would teach the elements of Prussian discipline to the motley rabble fighting for freedom. They would become an effective military force. If we are to rank men according to the value of their services in the American Revolution, after Washington none stand taller than von Steuben. He was the creator and molder of our nation's regular army.

GENTLEMAN JOHNNY

At about the same time Baron von Steuben was catering to German royalty, members of the posh Brook's Club in London, England were gathered around an open betting book as a handsome, ruddy-complexioned gentleman recorded a new entry which read: "John Burgoyne wagers Charles Fox fifty guineas that he will be home victorious from America by Christmas Day 1777."[1]

"Gentleman Johnny" had good reason for such flamboyant optimism. As early as the summer of 1775, Burgoyne had written the British government to suggest a grand campaign to divide and conquer the American colonies. He proposed: "A large army of such foreign troops as might be hired to begin their operations up the Hudson River from New York; another army composed partly of old disciplined troops and partly of Canadians, to act from Canada; a large levy of Indians conjointly with a detachment of regulars; and a numerous fleet to sweep the whole coast might possibly do the business in one campaign."

Major General Burgoyne took these opinions back with him to London during his winter leave in 1776, and elaborated on them further in a detailed document entitled "Thoughts for Conducting the War From the Side of Canada,"[2] a proposal for a Spring 1777 offensive along the Lake Champlain-Lake George route to Albany.

Burgoyne had superb political connections to the court. He was married to the daughter of the Earl of Derby and was himself a member of the House of Commons. He was also a part-time poet and playwright and loved games of sport and chance. The Crown decided to gamble on Burgoyne as the plan was readily approved, and the general received a commission to put the scheme into action. On May 7, 1777, the ship bearing General Burgoyne dropped anchor in Montreal.

Burgoyne's strategy was basically valid though it was complex in its timing and coordination. With a strong force, Burgoyne would sweep south, capture Fort Ticonderoga, and lead a drive on Albany. Burgoyne would come under Gen. William Howe's command, and a line of communication and cooperation would be established. Any significant American military presence in the colony of New York would be decimated and New England would be sealed off from the rest of the revolt. The source for tons of supplies and thousands of men for the rebellion would be eradicated.

ST. LEGER TAKES COMMAND

Burgoyne's plan also called for a third column, composed of British regulars, Hessians, Loyalists, and Indians, to come down the Mohawk River from the base at Oswego on Lake Ontario as a diversionary effort, and link up with Burgoyne in Albany. This mixed body of troops was put under the command of Lt. Col. Barry St. Leger. Born in 1737, St. Leger was a

British officer of Huguenot descent and a nephew of the fourth Viscount Doneraile. He brought to the campaign of 1777 an extensive military background. In 1756, he had entered the army as an ensign of the 28th Foot serving under General Abercrombie after his regiment was sent to America. During the French and Indian War, he had gained a reputation as a solid leader in frontier warfare. He had participated in the siege of Louisburg and was with Wolfe during the capture of Quebec. During this concluding chapter in the British conquest of Canada, St. Leger behaved gallantly near a bridge on the Charles River, helping to cut off the retreat of the French fugitives from the Plains of Abraham. He was slightly wounded in this engagement.

In 1762, he was promoted to major of the 95th Foot. St. Leger married the widow Lady Mansel in 1773 and two years later, after the outbreak of the American Revolution, was made lieutenant colonel of the 34th Foot.

On June 2, 1777, Barry St. Leger formally took command of his assorted expeditionary force which would number approximately 1,700 men when all the elements joined together at Oswego. It has been recorded that his detachment was composed of approximately the following units:

100 men from the 8th Regiment of Foot
100 men from the 34th Regiment of Foot
  87 Hesse Hanau jagers (light infantrymen)
  40 artillerymen with two 6-pounders, two 4-pounders, and four small mortars
133 men of the King's Royal Regiment of New York
100 Tory Rangers of the Indian Department
100 Canadian militiamen
1,000 Indian warriors

The Eighth, or "King's Regiment of Foot," had been stationed as garrison detachments along the Great Lakes at such places as Niagara and Detroit. The history of the regiment dates back to 1685 during the troubled reign of Charles I. It had seen service in the Battle of the Boyne, and under Queen Anne was designated as the "Queen's Regiment." It was one of the first units to storm the citadel of Liege in 1702, and two years later was involved in the epic victory at Blenheim. Upon the ascendance of George I as king, its designation was altered to the "Kings Regiment of Foot." Its uniform was scarlet red, with blue facing, and gold lace.

The 34th Foot was formed, in 1702, from enlistments in Norfolk, Essex, and adjacent counties. The 34th had arrived at Cape Fear in May 1776, and had since seen service in operations in Canada and Lake Champlain over the summer. This was Barry St. Leger's own regiment, and its uniform was red with pale yellow facing, and silver lace.

The Hesse-Hanau jager (rifle) company had been sent from its native land in the German state, landing in Canada in June 1777, and was immediately made part of St. Leger's command. Its commanding officer was a Lieutenant Hildebrand. The men of Hesse-Hanau had a rather unpleasant ship's voyage as the "men were packed like sardines" and the "pork and salt beef seemed five years old...the biscuits were full of maggots...and the water was all spoiled."[3]

The artillerymen manned guns which would prove to be too light to break down the defenses of any major fortification obstructing the advance of the expedition. There would be one such bastion of liberty in the direct path of St. Leger's attacking force—Fort Stanwix.

Soon after Sir John Johnson's arrival in Canada in the spring of 1776, he was given a colonel's commission and the authority to raise two battalions of one thousand Loyalist troops each. Of the paltry 283 men raised by Sir John's meager effort, 133 were assigned to him as part of St. Leger's column with the remaining one hundred fifty Loyalists under Maj. Ebenezer Jessup with Burgoyne's column. The popular name for Sir John's command was "Johnson's Royal Greens" because of the green color of their uniforms. The trim was white, the facing was orange, and the buttons were of pewter with the crown and letters "R.P." standing for "Royal Provincial" stamped on them. The leggings of the uniform were of brown cloth to the knee and the belts of buff leather were the same as in the regular British service. The military cocked hats of coarse felt were laced or bound with white tape. Two of the principal officers of Johnson's Royal Greens included Johnson's brother-in-law, Maj. Stephen Watts, and a Captain McDonald. Some of the Canadian militiamen with St. Leger's force would double as axe and bateaux men during the expedition.

On or about Saturday June 21, 1777, Lt. Col. Barry St. Leger's command began its movement down the St. Lawrence River to rendezvous at Buck Island at the entrance to Lake Ontario. Daniel Claus would join them there in the company of one hundred fifty Huron Indians. The plan was to link up with Butler's Tory Rangers and a large host of Iroquois allies at Oswego.

CONFERENCE AT UNADILLA

About one week after St. Leger and Sir John began boating down the St. Lawrence with their troops, Brig. Gen. Nicholas Herkimer, with an escort of one hundred fifty Tryon County militiamen, arrived at Unadilla for a conference with Mohawk leader, Joseph Brant, in an attempt to prevent the union of the Iroquois with the approaching Loyalist and British enemy. On June 27, 1777, the negotiations began. In 1845, historian William L. Stone interviewed a witness to the meeting, Joseph Wagner of Fort Plain. Wagner stated that at the meeting Brant was attended by three other Mohawk leaders including William Johnson, the Indian son of Sir William. Brant boasted that he had "five hundred warriors under his command and could in an instant destroy the small Patriot party, but because Herkimer was an old neighbor, he would not."[4] At this, Col. Ebenezer Cox and Brant began exchanging sarcastic remarks. Herkimer interrupted to assure the Mohawk Chief that his intentions were peaceable.

Brant reservedly asked General Herkimer the object of his visit, which the brigadier made known to be a desire to secure a pledge of neutrality on the part of the Six Nations as the flames of war made their way to the Mohawk Valley. Herkimer's mission would not, however, bear fruit with the Mohawks or their sister nations of the Onondoga, Cayuga, or Seneca. The previous spring, at council sessions held at Niagara, Col. John Butler had already received their promise of support for King George III to help the English quell the rebels.

Joseph Brant had already been fully won over to the English side during a visit to England in January of 1776. He had sailed with Guy Johnson, Daniel Claus, and young Walter Butler for an audience with Lord George Germain and His Majesty, George III at St. James Palace. Brant became a sincere admirer of King George even though he refused to kiss his hand on the grounds that he was an emissary of the Six Nations who were allies of the Crown, but not subjects. Years later Brant would say "I have had the honour to be introduced to the King of England... a finer man than whom I think it would be a truly difficult task to find."[5]

After Brant returned to America, he traveled among the people of the Six Nations encouraging them to aid his British comrades. He had a message to deliver to his people from the King of England. His Majesty's armies in Canada and New York would be making a juncture as soon as the weather permitted. The Iroquois Confederacy should prepare to cooperate with these military movements.

After three centuries the democratic system known as the Great Binding Law would be torn into shreds because Joseph Brant was not successful in convincing all of the tribes to join the British. Heeding counsel from Samuel Kirkland and their own tribal leaders, most of the Oneida Nation and the adopted Tuscaroras maintained their neutrality. Soon they would emerge as America's first allies in war. The covenant chain would be irrevocably broken on the battlefield at Oriskany.

COUNCIL AT OSWEGO

On July 25, 1777, St. Leger's military column reached Fort Oswego. At Three Rivers, where the Oneida and Seneca Rivers merged to form the Oswego, most of the warriors of the Six Nations were waiting for them. There were almost a thousand fighting men. The English came bearing gifts including fresh beef and intoxicating drinks. As the Indians feasted, John Butler, Daniel Claus, Joseph Brant, and even St. Leger urged the warriors to join the expedition. Not all were convinced. Finally, Claus got a brilliant idea. He told the braves, "Go with us and watch us whip the rebels. Sit down and smoke your pipes and see what a grand show we will provide." This brought about almost unanimous consent among the warriors. St. Leger had just doubled the size of his attacking legion. A Seneca chief recalled, "Our chiefs began to think that the Great Britain government is very rich and powerful to his dominion to force things and kind to his Nation."[6]

News of the approaching enemy juggernaut reached the Patriots by way of the Oneida Indians, creating panic in the Mohawk Valley. A letter sent by the chairman of the Albany Committee of Safety to Gen. Philip Schuyler illustrates the concern:

"Honorable Sir—Col. Vrooman and two other gentlemen from Schoharie are now with us, and represent the distress their part of the country is driven to. Threats, they hourly receive; their persons and property are exposed to imminent danger; nearly one half of the people heretofore well disposed, have laid down their arms, and propose to side with the enemy. All which change has taken its origin from the desertion of Ticonderoga, the unprecedented loss of which, we are afraid, will be followed by a revolt of more than half of the northern part of this county."[7]

On August 2, 1777, Brig. Gen. Nicholas Herkimer was sent a communique from provincial governor, George Clinton, with instructions as to why a draft of militia was necessary.

"Sir, The small number of Continental troops occupying the western posts renders it necessary to raise a reinforcement from the Militia in your Brigade. Upon the receipt hereof you will therefore, without delay detach five hundred men and cause them to be posted at the most suitable passes in your County for giving protection to the inhabitants against the incursions of the enemy and for reinforcing the garrisons in your quarter.... I need not direct you to use expedition; your exposed Frontier and nearness to a cruel enemy will induce you to fall upon the most effectual measures for carrying these orders into immediate execution...."[8]

Unbeknown to Clinton, Herkimer realized the imminent danger and had already taken decisive action by issuing a proclamation on July 17 announcing that two thousand "Christians and savages" had assembled at Oswego for a descent upon the Mohawk Valley and had warned the entire adult male population to be ready at a moment's notice to take the field in fighting fashion. All men from "sixteen to sixty"[9] were required for active service while the aged and infirm would defend the women and children at designated strong points in the valley. On July 30, the blacksmith Thomas Spencer, who resided with the Oneidas, warned the militia that in just a few days the enemy would arrive in their vicinity. He was correct, for St. Leger's destination was Fort Stanwix, an American occupied garrison in the valley wilderness.

FORT STANWIX

In 1758, following the de Lery raid on Fort Bull near the Oneida Carry, a portage road between Wood Creek and the Mohawk River, the British decided to reoccupy the carry and build a larger fort that could withstand the type of attack made on Fort Bull. Work on what would become Fort Stanwix began in the fall of that year with the permission of the Oneida Indians.

The structure was named for Brig. Gen. John Stanwix who commanded the troops on the carry. Over 2,500 troops worked on the fort, digging ditches and hewing logs, but disease took a toll on the men and the actual number of the effective work force at one time was usually far less. By winter, the fort was sufficiently erected to house four hundred men of Britain's 71st Regiment of Foot, Fraser's Highlanders.

The fortress contained five casemates, a grouping of officer's huts on the parade ground, and a powder magazine in the northwest bombproof. Entrance to the fort was gained over a causeway and a row of pickets was placed in the ditch surrounding the fort. By the summer of 1759, the work was fundamentally completed.

The English abandoned Fort Stanwix following the Treaty of 1768. It was not occupied again until the outbreak of the American Revolution. In the summer of 1776, Continental troops from Connecticut and New Jersey occupied the carry and began rebuilding the dilapidated fort. The work was continued in the spring of 1777 by the men of the 3rd New York Regiment.

This unit's twenty-eight-year-old commander arrived on May 3, 1777, with a portion of his command. His name was Peter Gansevoort. Colonel Gansevoort was a bit over six feet in height and well-built. He was methodical, exacting and, by gracious upbringing, a courteous man. He attended the College of New Jersey at Princeton and was a veteran of Gen. Richard Montgomery's ill-fated Patriot invasion of Canada. In the 3rd New York Regiment, he had inherited a formation deficient in numbers and provisions. He successfully overcame these challenges by aggressively recruiting men and procuring supplies.

Gansevoort's second-in-command, Lt. Col. Marinus Willett, would prove to be equally effective. Willett was born in Jamaica, New York on July 31, 1740, one of thirteen children. He spent his youth in New York City where his father operated a famous inn, located in the former De-Lancey Mansion, known as the Province Arms.

Willett was commissioned as a second lieutenant during the French and Indian War and, like St. Leger, served under Generals James Abercrombie and George Howe in the failed Fort Ticonderoga Campaign of 1758. He also marched with Colonel Bradstreet against Fort Frontenac on Lake Ontario.

As the war with France dwindled to a close, Willett married Mary Pearsee at Trinity Church in New York City. They had a son in 1761 and named him after his father. The seeds of Willett's Patriot sympathies were sown years before, during the trial of Peter Zenger.

A young lawyer named John Morin Scott had formed the Sons of Liberty. After the British Parliament had passed the Stamp Act in 1765, Scott wrote in the New York Gazette these inflammatory words: "The great fundamental principles of government should be common to all its parts and members, else the whole will be endangered. If, then, the interest of the mother country and her colonies cannot be made to coincide...then the connection between them ought to cease; and sooner or later, it must inevitably cease."[10] Young Marinus Willett agreed with him, much to the dismay of Willett's Loyalist father.

When in September 1769, the Sons of Liberty began to rise in revolt, Willett helped to print placards to announce the raising of a liberty pole which was inscribed "The King, Pitt and Liberty." A scuffle later ensued between the Sons of Liberty and British soldiers garrisoned in the city, with Willett right in the middle of the melee.

By 1775, the fields of Massachusetts had been stained with Patriot's blood and in New York City British troops were in the process of moving arms and accoutrements through the streets. As the long procession of carts protected by redcoats came down Broad Street, a single figure stood in the way blocking the intersection. It was Marinus Willett. Jumping up on the first cart, Marinus appealed to the soldiers. "You are the tools of a despot. Come over to our side. Enjoy the air of freedom."[11] On May 28, 1777, this heroic freedom fighter marched with the remainder of the 3rd NY Regiment into Fort Stanwix.

Beginning on June 25, 1777, perilous incidents escalated in the vicinity of Fort Stanwix as independent war parties of Iroquois began to reconnoiter the garrison's perimeter. On this June day Captain Gregg and Corporal Maddeson were about one and a quarter mile from the fort when they were attacked by a party of Indians who tomahawked and scalped them. The captain would survive his injury but Corporal Maddeson was dead.

On July 3, Ensign Sporr was in command of six men cutting sod for the garrison, when they were surprised by an Indian band who killed and scalped one, scalped and wounded another, and took the ensign and four men prisoner.

On July 27, a group of American sentinels rushed from their posts in an attempt to save three young girls out picking raspberries. The girls, who belonged to families living at Fort Stanwix for protection, were only two hundred yards from the fort's pickets when they were fired upon and scalped by Indians waiting in hiding. When the Patriot men reached the fallen girls, two were already dead and one was wounded.

As the tearful soldiers carried the limp bodies back inside the fort, a somber hush fell over all who witnessed the tragic procession. If there had been any doubts before, the harsh reality of the bloodied rag-doll forms vividly reminded the onlookers that the terror and bitterness of war had come to the Mohawk Valley. Beyond this solitary blockade in the wilderness nestled the homes and families of many of these men.

The next day Colonel Gansevoort sent away those women and children belonging to the garrison. In a letter sent to Colonel Van Schaik the same day, Gansevoort would write, "...these mercenaries of Britain came not to fight, but to lie in wait to murder; and it is equally the same to them, if they can get a scalp, whether it is from a soldier or an innocent babe."[12]

On July 30, Major Bedlam arrived with one hundred fifty men from Colonel Wesson's Massachusetts Regiment. On August 1, three Oneida Indians came to the fort to warn the Americans that they had seen at least one hundred strange Indians in the area. The next day, the military complement of Fort Stanwix was completed with the arrival of Lieutenant Colonel Mellon and one hundred men of the Massachusetts Regiment along with four bateaux filled with valuable supplies.

Colonel Gansevort's force now numbered seven hundred fifty men composed of the following elements:

450 soldiers of Gansevoort's 3rd New York Line Regiment

250 soldiers of Wesson's Massachusetts Regiment

50 New York State Militiamen

The last of the Massachusetts men were barely inside the fort when the report of gunfire was heard from the direction of the landing. Two of the bateaux men were wounded, one was captured, and one was missing. The missing bateaux man was later found shot through the head, stabbed in the chest, and scalped. Though he was miraculously alive when discovered, he died a short time later.

THE SIEGE BEGINS

On Sunday August 3, 1777, the advance party of Lt. Col. Barry St. Leger's expeditionary force, composed of a small group of English troops and Indians under Lieutenant Bird, appeared out of the woods and invested the fort. The siege of Fort Stanwix had officially begun.

At 3 o'clock in the afternoon, St. Leger sent Capt. Gilbert Tice, under a flag of truce, to the fort. Captain Tice was admitted, blindfolded, and escorted to Gansevoort and Willett. He brought with him a proclamation from St. Leger. Tice told the garrison that, "The unnatural rebellion had been made a foundation for the completest system of tyranny that ever God in his displeasure suffered for a time to be exercised over a froward and stubborn generation."

Tortures and imprisonment were being inflicted by assemblies calling themselves friends of liberty. Religion was being profaned. Multitudes were being compelled to swear allegiance to a power they abhorred. The English captain said St. Leger brought succor "to those whose spirit and principle may induce to partake the glorious task of redeeming their countrymen from dungeons and reestablishing the blessings of legal government."

He also threatened to those who resisted His Majesty's forces that "the messengers of justice and of wrath await them in the field and devastation, famine and every concomitant horror that a reluctant but indispensable prosecution of military must occasion, will bar the way to their return."[13] Gansevoort curtly dismissed Tice. He was ushered to the main gate and his blindfold was removed. He disappeared into the woods to report to his commander.

When St. Leger came up with his main contingent to surround the fort he had a good view of Peter Gansevoort's reply. Instead of a docile white flag of surrender, a defiant continental flag flew bravely over the ramparts. Later Gansevoort would write: "It is my determined resolution to defend this fort and garrison to the last extremity, in behalf of the United American States, who have placed me here to defend it against all their enemies."[14]

HERKIMER TAKES ACTION

Over forty miles away, another American officer was also answering his country's call. At the news of St. Leger's investment of Fort Stanwix, Brig. Gen. Nicholas Herkimer had immediately summoned the Tryon County Militia to action. The patriots mustered at Fort Dayton, the present-day village of Herkimer, in rapid concentration. The brigade was composed mostly of farmers, but many tradesmen, woodsmen, and members of the political committee also responded to Herkimer's orders. On August 3, eight hundred came to Fort Dayton to repel the invaders.

From head to toe the militiamen were clothed and equipped in a motley collection of articles. Many wore the military cocked hat, but others had round hats or flopped hats made of black felt. Many of the round variety were accented by a bucktail feather and/or cockade. There were also knitted liberty caps and fox or raccoon fur hats. Some dressed in shirts of white linen with ruffles below the collar, some added waistcoats. Others were more comfortable in a rifle or hunting shirt or frock made of linen or deerskin, with cape and fringe. A few had regimental coats from previous military service worn as a symbol of rank or put on civilian overcoats, depending on the climatic conditions.

Their breeches were generally made of linen or wool broadcloth and were usually white or buff in color. The breeches were laced at the waistband for a good fit. There were men in overalls and trousers made of linen, cotton, or wool broadcloth. On the lower part of their legs, some strapped on half-gaiters made of heavy black linen or cotton.

They wore shoes of leather with square or oval brass buckles. Many of the woodsmen wore deerskin moccasins laced with leather thongs. Some of the moccasins were decorated with beads in the Indian tradition. Many wore stockings of loosely loomed linen, wool, or cotton. Their clothing was adorned with buttons of bone, wood, pewter, or brass.

The Tryon County Militia Brigade's essential equipment for waging war was more standardized. Every militiaman was required to own a musket when serving in the state militia. Most of the soldiers were equipped with the standard British .75 caliber Brown Bess musket or an American copy fitted with a sixteen-inch bayonet The State Committee of Safety had contracted with local gunsmiths to reproduce this popular firearm to augment those already in the province or captured from the British. A few unfortunate men may have carried the "Militiaman's Fowler," a weapon which was a thrifty mix of parts from worn-out weapons. Rarely was this piece fitted with a bayonet.

The troops would carry their ammunition in hunting bags holding the priming horn, lead balls, and extra flints. The powder was held in horns removed from oxen and cattle. Sometimes they were decoratively engraved to uniquely identify the owner. The cartridges were carried at the waist in a cartridge box or tin canister which was popular because it was waterproof.

Firing the musket was a time-consuming, thirteen-step process. The sequence was: 1. Half cock firelock; 2. Handle cartridge; 3. Prime; 4. Shut pan; 5. Charge with cartridge; 6. Draw ramrod; 7. Ram down cartridge; 8. Return ramrod; 9. Shoulder firelock; 10 Poise firelock; 11. Cock firelock; 12. Take aim; 13. Fire!

A competent militiaman could perform these actions in under thirty seconds, but the slow-loading of the piece and the fact that he had no means of attaching a bayonet while in the process of loading, could create a calamitous situation when the enemy was bearing down. Often a single rifle shot was all that stood between the rifleman and certain death. For this reason, the soldier would also carry other personal side arms including tomahawks, hunting knives, and pistols. Swords and spontoons were often carried by officers as a symbol of their authority. Halberds, a throwback to the Middle Ages, sometimes were carried by sergeants and corporals, not so much as a weapon but as a badge of rank. Militiamen lacking a bayonet would often supplement their main firearm with a trench pike, which gave them the ability to evade a lunging bayonet.

To slake their thirst along the line of march and in the heat of battle, the troops would carry wooden or tin canteens. Food, clothing, and blankets were carried in knapsacks and haversacks slung over their shoulders.

The command structure of the brigade had changed since August of the year before. When Herkimer was commissioned as brigadier, Colonel Cox succeeded him as head of the Canajoharie Regiment. The Tory sympathies of Herkimer's brother, Han Yost, colonel of the 4th Battalion, had been uncovered and he had since fled to Canada. Han Yost Herkimer joined St. Leger's column opposing his own brother. Peter Bellinger was named to fill the position of Colonel of the 4th Battalion.

The command structure of the Tryon County Militia now was:

Brig. Gen. Nicholas Herkimer
Brig. Maj. John Frey
Brig. Surgeon Moses Younglove
1st Battalion, Canajoharie Regt., Col. Ebenezer Cox
Lt. Col. William Seeber, 1st Maj. Samuel Campbell

2nd Maj. Samuel Clyde, Quartermaster John Pickard
2nd Battalion, Palatine Regt., Col. Jacob Klock
Lt. Col. Peter Wagner, First Maj. Harmanus Van Slyke
2nd Maj. Isaac Paris, Adj. Anthony Van Vechten
3rd Battalion, Mohawk Regt., Col. Frederick Visscher
Lt. Col. Volkert Veeder, 1st Maj. John Bliven
2nd Maj. John Newkirk, Adj. Peter Conyne
4th Battalion, Kingsland-German Flatts Regt., Col. Peter Bellinger
Lt. Col. Frederick Bellinger, 1st Maj. John Eisenlord
2nd Maj. Augustus Clapsaddle, Surgeon William Petry.

THE MILITIA MOVES

On the morning of August 4, 1777, serenaded by the fife and drum, the eight hundred men of the Tryon County Militia Brigade began their line of march from Fort Dayton. Their objective—the relief of Fort Stanwix. Accompanying the half-mile-long column were over forty oxcarts and wagons carrying ammunition and provisions. To give his force better tactical flexibility and to maintain the speed of his advance, General Herkimer established a depot at Deerfield, leaving all but fifteen of the wagons with a detachment of forty militiamen. This would leave the brigadier with an effective force of approximately 760 soldiers.

Herkimer's men confidently marched while, at the same time, Gen. George Washington was sending a letter to the Council of Safety from his headquarters in Philadelphia.

> "The misfortune of Ticonderoga has produced a very disagreeable alteration to our affairs, and has thrown a gloom upon the favorable prospect, which the campaign, previous to that event, afforded. But I am in great hopes, the ill consequences of it will shortly subside in the minds of the people of your State and give way to the more rational dictates of self-preservation and regard to the common good. But while people continue to view what has happened through the medium of supineness or fear, there is no saying to what length an enterprising genius may push his good fortune."[15]

"Self-preservation" and "the common good," Washington had written. Surely these were both motivating factors in the minds of the immortal eight hundred and their brigadier as they lay awake on the ground at Staring Creek, their encampment the night of August 4. The only obstacles to St. Leger's pillaging force, one which would obliterate their hearths and families, were Fort Stanwix and this militia. They rallied together for "the common good" as the cycle of history represented by the devastation of their ancestral homes in the Palatinate threatened to repeat itself.

Twenty-six miles to go. At the crack of dawn they were on the move again along "bad roads through thick woods." The column crossed the Great Ford of the Mohawk and wheeled to the west. They made camp the night of August 5 near the Oneida Indian village of Oriska, meaning "Field of Nettles."

Earlier in the day General Herkimer had sent three of his scouts, Adam Helmer, Han Marks Demuth, and Hon Yost Folts, to Fort Stanwix with orders to make Colonel Gansevoort aware of the strength of his relief force. He also requested that Gansevoort send out an ample military sortie to rendezvous with the militia. Between their two forces, they could severely disrupt the enemy siege. In his letter Herkimer suggested that Gansevoort signal support was on its way by firing three sequential cannon shots. His plans in proper order, Nicholas Herkimer slumbered.

Others in the final encampment were not so restful. Whispered conversations continued all night long between senior officers, their subordinates and some members of the political body, the Tryon County Committee of Safety. Some of the junior officers were not content to recline in comfort so close to their sworn enemies.

A hot and humid day greeted General Herkimer as he arose in the morning. The forty-nine-year-old brigadier surveyed the men with pride and satisfaction as he puffed on his clay pipe. These were his people. Side by side he had cleared the land with them to carve out a new life in the wilderness. He had held many of the younger officers in his arms as infants. Nicholas and Maria Herkimer had no sons or daughters. These bright young men assembled before him were his "children."

All the more reason why Nicholas Herkimer must have been shocked by the bickering of his officers at a morning conference called to discuss the orders of the day and review the plan arranged with Peter Gansevoort. Col. Ebenezer Cox was against waiting for a signal from the fort to advance. Cox egged on the impulsive and impatient younger officers, some of whom insisted the militia should advance now and not wait for any "damned signal."

There had been bad blood between Herkimer and Cox since the time when the Herkimer family had Cox's father, Julian, arrested for nonpayment of debt. Herkimer, however, having survived the French and Indian War and having saved many lives as a military commander, had developed the good sense to know when to exercise restraint. He sensed that this was one of those times and that the brigade should wait for the signal from Gansevoort.

Herkimer's brother-in-law, Colonel Bellinger, supported his sentiments, but the other colonels, old Jacob Klock and Frederick Visscher, were silent. Finally, Cox made comments regarding Herkimer's Tory brother and inferred that perhaps Nicholas' patriotic loyalty was also not all it should be. Cox crossed the line when he said, "I will not wait for a coward." This was too much for the proud brigadier. Striding to his white horse, he mounted, drew his sword, and pointed to the west, "Vorwaerts!" he roared as the pipe fell out of his mouth. There was a mad scramble to assemble the troops as the command "Forward!" echoed throughout the camp.[16]

As a smug Ebenezer Cox brushed past the general, Herkimer exclaimed, "A few hours will tell us which are the brave." Perhaps the moment after Gen. Nicholas Herkimer uttered the command to march on he regretted it. As his horse plodded forward, two thoughts may have swirled through his brain. "To what cursed fate am I leading my children and neighbors?" and "How can I stall for more time?"

It was 10 A.M., August 6, 1777—only a couple of miles to go.

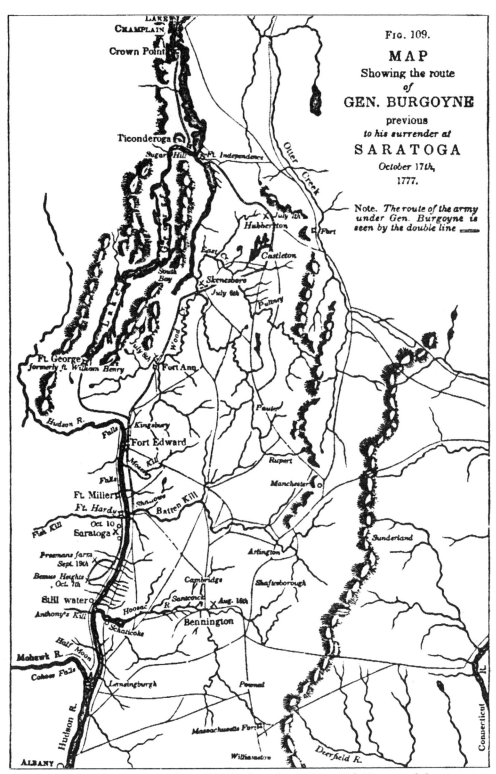

Burgoyne's plan for the Campaign of 1777, from Lee's *Pictorial History of the American Revolution,* collection of the Oneida County Historical Society

Soldier of the British 34th Regiment of Foot in 1776, illustration by David Yahnke

Lt. Col. Barry St. Leger, illustration by David Yahnke

Herkimer negotiating with Brant at Unadilla, courtesy of the National Park Service, Fort Stanwix National Monument

Peter Gansevoort, from Simms'
Trappers of New York, collection
of the Utica Public Library

Marinus Willett, from
Thomas' *Marinus Willett*

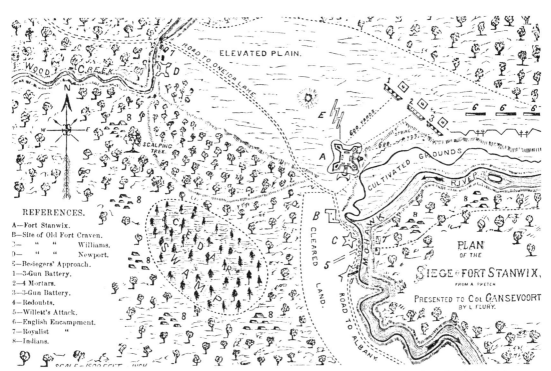

REFERENCES.

A—Fort Stanwix.
B—Site of Old Fort Craven.
C— " " Williams.
D— " " Newport.
E—Besiegers' Approach.
1—3-Gun Battery.
2—4 Mortars.
3—3-Gun Battery.
4—Redoubts.
5—Willett's Attack.
6—English Encampment.
7—Royalist "
8—Indians.

Plan of the Siege of Fort Stanwix, from Simms' *Frontiersmen of New York*, collection of the Utica Public Library

The militia column crossing the Great Ford of the Mohawk on August 5, illustration by David Yahnke

Muster at Fort Dayton on August 4, illustration by David Yahnke

The conference on the morning of August 6, illustration by David Yahnke

"Forward!" illustration by David Yahnke

I will face the enemy.
—*Nicholas Herkimer*
10:30 A.M., Wednesday, Sixth of August 1777

Chapter Seven

THE BATTLE

"The Battle of Oriskany," by Frederick Yohn, courtesy of the Utica Public Library

About two miles west of Oriska and six miles from Fort Stanwix is a series of undulating slopes. At the base of many of these small hills run narrow streams feeding into the Mohawk River to the north. The plunging ravines along the banks of these creeks tend to be marshy and, therefore, the ground is moist in these areas.

Winding through this region was the Military Road, or King's Highway, built in 1758 as a route to Fort Stanwix. Logs were placed along the road at creek crossings and in the damp earth of the ravine to facilitate the movement of troops and supply wagons. Brig. Gen. Nicholas Herkimer would have known this road well. As a Captain of Militia, he had helped to construct it nineteen years before.

The Military Road was at least sixteen feet in width—enough distance to allow two wagons to pass each other without difficulty. The road sliced through the virgin forest which surrounded it. Some records indicate that a terrific storm had cut a swath through this region just a few weeks before. Many of the trees had been blown down, creating natural fortifications for any combat contingent choosing to take advantage of the situation.

A column of soldiers and wagons moving through such inhospitable terrain would be the military equivalent of entering the mouth of hell, if the enemy chose to avail themselves of such a splendid opportunity. This was the environment that Nicholas Herkimer and the Tryon County Militia Brigade found themselves plodding through at ten A.M. on the morning of August 6, 1777.

The long column stretched over half a mile, rolling across two slopes intersected by two damp ravines with corresponding babbling brooks. The day had dawned extraordinarily hot and the air was thick with humidity. The perspiring militiamen loosened their clothing accordingly. Most of the men bantered enthusiastically, marched in ranks of two or three, excited to be on the move once again. Nicholas Herkimer did not share in their merriment, silently trotting ahead in the company of his old 1st Battalion Canajoharie comrades, his brow furrowed deep in thought. If the boisterous soldiers had ceased their idle chatter, if only for a moment, they may have noticed that an eerie silence hung over the forest.

The formation was led by an advance guard of about twenty men who were scouting along the road around one hundred yards forward of the main body. Spotting the inviting stream below, the tired and dusty scouts lumbered down the slope of the western ravine, dropped their muskets, dipped their heads into the cool water, and quenched their thirst.

Behind the vanguard a gloating Col. Ebenezer Cox led his 1st Battalion across the highlands of the western heights, still tingling with the excitement of his triumph of will over Herkimer. The lieutenant colonel of the

Canajoharie boys was William Seeber. This talented officer would need all of his considerable leadership ability on this day.

The 1st Battalion was followed appropriately enough by the troops of the 2nd Battalion, Palatine Regiment commanded by Jacob Klock. Klock was the oldest senior officer in the column this morning and an original member of the Palatine District Committee of Safety. The sixty-nine-year-old battalion leader relied heavily on the youthful energy of the formation's lieutenant colonel, Peter Wagner.

The 2nd Battalion preceded the 4th Battalion composed of men from the Kingsland and German Flatts District. The 4th's colonel was Nicholas Herkimer's brother-in-law, Peter Bellinger. He was about the same age as Herkimer and a strong supporter of the brigadier. The position of lieutenant colonel was filled by Frederick Bellinger, Peter's cousin. Later, under duress, Frederick would waver in his loyalty to the cause.

It is likely that the sixty Oneida Indians that joined with the militia on their march would have been with the men of Kingsland/German Flatts. Because of the proximity of the district to the Oneida villages, the Native Americans were most familiar with these neighbors and quite comfortable in their company. These stalwart allies included the Oneida war chief, Han Yerry Doxtater (Tewahangaraghkan), who came with his son and young wife on horseback and Thomas Spencer, the blacksmith who had warned the militia of the impending arrival of St. Leger's invading force. There was a sturdy fellow named Louis (Atyataronghta), who was from the St. Regis region. All of these courageous warriors would prove their friendship to the Patriots on this fateful morning. Blatcop would also serve the militia well.

Behind the 4th Battalion were fifteen oxcarts, which at 10 A.M. were just entering the eastern ravine. It is believed that the fifteen wagons with the Tryon County Militia Brigade were either farm wagons and/or oxcarts. Ten of these wagons were filled with food provisions, enough to sustain the brigade for two more days. Five of the wagons carried the ammunition, including a replenishment of cannonballs for the guns at Fort Stanwix.

The rear guard of the column was now situated on the eastern heights overlooking the ravine and the stream later known as Battle Creek. This tail of the force was the 3rd Battalion composed of men from the Mohawk District. Their commanding officer was Col. Frederick Visscher.

Visscher was born in 1741 in Albany. With his wife, Gazena, he had seven children. His thoughts may have been with them as he surveyed the ravine below and the crude causeway across the creek.

As Visscher was also in charge of the baggage wagons, he noted with concern the "causey" extending across the creek bed and marshy banks.

This culvert was constructed of poles tied together into bundles, placed crosswise on the road, and covered with earth. This allowed water to seep across the road below instead of across the surface. The colonel surmised the wagons, which were now entering the ravine, would have no problem navigating the crossing.

Later, Visscher and his second-in-command, Lt. Col. Volkert Veeder, may have wished they had directed more attention to the conduct of their troops instead of the oxen; their leadership of the 3rd Battalion on this morning of infamy would be called into question by a body politic seeking a scapegoat.

The militia's General Herkimer must have been fuming inside and was probably cursing the insubordination of Cox and angry at his own explosive and impetuous act of rage. Yet, perhaps, there remained a slim chance of preserving the precious lives of his dear friends. Time was what he needed. If the boys of the vanguard paused to fill their parched throats with the soothing natural liquid of the stream, so be it. If Visscher experienced difficulty and delay in bringing those wagons across the causeway, this was useful, and if other officers in that column, perhaps privy or sensitive to Herkimer's misgivings, chose this critical moment to temporarily bring their detachments to a halt and order a formal inspection of the troops, the general would be grateful.

Nicholas Herkimer was a pious, gentle man. The humble brigadier may have silently prayed to his God to forgive him for his anger and to grant him an interval of time for the sake of his men. He implored his Creator to stir the conscious thoughts of Peter Gansevoort to bring about the sound of three cannons booming in echoing succession. More than anything at this moment, the general probably longed to hear the sweet refrain of artillery from the direction of Fort Stanwix. What he heard instead, emanating from the bowels of the western ravine up ahead, were the sounds he most dreaded, the crackling of musketry, the shrieking of terrified souls, and the piercing war whoops of the Iroquois.

Early in the evening of August 5, a Mohawk runner had raced into the bivouac perimeter of Lt. Col. Barry St. Leger's headquarters. He came with a vital message from Molly Brant, now at her home in Canajoharie, and serving as the eyes and ears of the Crown's forces in the midst of their enemy. The rebel militia was on the move! And they were headed in the direction of the British besieging Fort Stanwix. A scout confirmed this information.

St. Leger immediately called a conference of his staff officers and the Iroquois and Loyalist leaders. At about the same time that Cox and his co-conspirators began plotting against General Herkimer, St. Leger proposed a plan to foil the militia initiative.

A substantial force of Iroquois, Loyalist rangers, and the King's Royal Regiment of New York would be sent under the direction of Joseph Brant, Sir John Johnson, and John Butler to lay an ambuscade at a suitable location along the rebels' line of march. Sir John would be the titular head of the composite command, but Brant would select the place of ambush because of his keen familiarity with the region. Most of the men would look to the charismatic Mohawk chieftain, because of his natural leadership capabilities. It is unknown at this time how the Iroquois chiefs were convinced to participate in the ambush.

The Iroquois, primarily Seneca and Mohawk warriors, would make up the bulk of the formation. Working in conjunction with one hundred rangers, they would amass five hundred braves in all, the younger warriors eager to wash their spears and tomahawks in the blood of the enemy. The Seneca chiefs Cornplanter, Old Smoke, the young Red Jacket, and Black Snake would be present. So would William Johnson of Canajoharie. There would also be one hundred men of Johnson's Royal Greens, all but the light infantry company would act as a reserve column to move onto the field, after the trap was sprung, as a final thrust to finish the brutal task begun by the Indians and rangers.

A smattering of historians place the Hessian jagers under Lieutenant Hildebrand with this force, but if they were there, they played a minor role. Some accounts cite Daniel Claus as a participant with the rangers, but Claus himself later denied it.

There was one Tory leader who voiced dissent with the plan. Col. John Butler suggested that perhaps an attempt should be made to parlay with the militia officers in the hope of convincing them of the error of their rebel ideology. Butler must have felt regret at the two armies' impending collision course to prompt such a suggestion. It was one thing to have an unpleasant political disagreement with your former neighbors and constituents. It was quite another to spill their blood.

Joseph Brant dismissed Butler's recommendation in a curt manner. The time for diplomacy had passed. The die was cast. The time for a decisive military resolution had arrived.

A second scout arrived in St. Leger's camp. The militia was at Oriska, only a few miles away. The conference was concluded and, in the dark of the pre-dawn hours of August 6, St. Leger stood and sternly gazed at the shadowy forms of the seven hundred men as they quietly slipped into the woods heading to the east where the enemy slumbered unaware.

Joseph Brant surveyed the ground he had selected with a nod of approval. The undulating slopes and precipitous swampy ravines in between were perfect for the ambuscade. The Iroquois Indians and most of the rangers were arranged in a fishhook pattern extending to the slopes beyond the western ravine and sweeping down both sides flanking the western heights. Brant, with sixty of the Mohawks and twenty rangers, was positioned on the southern heights facing the eastern ravine. The thick forest would conceal the entire host from the vision of the slow moving militia snaking along the road. When the last of the rebels' rear guard had submerged themselves in the abyss of the eastern ravine, Brant would blow the shrill sound of a ranger's signal whistle. This would alert the force along the line to initiate the onslaught.

The main attacking force's planned tactics would not be unlike the famous Zulu "horns of the bull" formation at Isandlwana one hundred and two years later. The primary Iroquois and ranger detachments, composed of five hundred twenty men, would flank both sides of the thinly-stretched militia column, drawing the disorganized enemy toward the center of the formation of one hundred soldiers of Johnson's Royal Greens, where the militia would meet a solid phalanx of belching musket fire.

At the same time, Brant's eighty-man contingent would swiftly rush down from the southern heights and seal off any avenue of escape for the opposing troops and capture their baggage train. The entire militia would be trapped and gradually ground down to the point of obliteration or surrender. It seemed a foolproof scheme.

Earlier in the day, an Iroquois scout had been carefully hidden in a causeway to the east so as to give Brant prior warning of the militia brigade's proximity, and to attempt a head count. When he reported back, Brant, Butler, and Johnson were ecstatic to learn that the enemy's column was smaller than the initial estimate of one thousand troops. They were also sadly informed of the presence of Oneida warriors with the brigade.

All was in readiness. Seven hundred armed men lay concealed in the dense cover of the wilds surrounding the King's Highway. A Quebec militia captain with St. Leger's force, Hertel DeRoville, would poetically describe it this way: "And on the field we set up an ambush. In a spot along side of their road, where the woods almost completely surrounded us. Everyone crouched like birds sitting on eggs. Or if you prefer, like a she-wolf who, when she sees a timid and defenseless animal coming at a rapid pace, lies in wait for it and with a light leap, strikes it, kills it and leaves it in pieces."[1]

And then they came. Brant watched as the vanguard appeared on the road on the eastern heights followed shortly by the lead elements of the 1st Battalion led by his old adversary Ebenezer Cox. Soon he spied Herkimer plodding forward on his white steed. Just six weeks before, Joseph Brant had sat across a conference table from Nicholas Herkimer. On this day, he must have thought, one of them would die. Then came the 2nd Battalion led by one of the hated Klocks, followed by the men of the 4th Battalion. Crossing the slopes and descending into the eastern ravine was Brant's prize, the supply wagons dragged by the powerful oxen clamped in their yokes.

The enemy's rear guard was just now marching across the eastern heights. Brant fingered his signal whistle nervously, just a few more minutes. The Mohawk chieftain was puzzled as certain company commanders in the 4th Battalion barked orders bringing their units to a standstill. The remainder of the column slowed down to a snail's pace behind them. Brant grew irritated. "Move, damn you!" he may have thought.

Suddenly Brant was startled by the sound of musket fire from the recesses of the western ravine beyond his vision. He then heard the distinctive war cry of his people, which had echoed through this wilderness for centuries. The trap was prematurely sprung! The militia column became a hornet's nest of activity.

For the brash young Iroquois warriors and chiefs positioned in front of the vanguard, many of them in their first major combat, the sight of this enemy reclining and filling themselves with the stream water, their weapons discarded uselessly on the ground, was too tempting a target to resist. With a whoop they rose from their hiding places, discharged their fire weapons, and rushed en masse among the helpless prone figures of the shocked scouts.

For the twenty "sacrificial lambs" of the advance guard, it was over in seconds. A militia private, Conrad Mowers, later remembered witnessing from some distance on the western heights, with horror, the slaying of three of the scouts. The Iroquois braves swarmed among them piercing their bodies with spears, severing limbs with tomahawks, and crushing skulls with war clubs. Miraculously, one man of the vanguard, Jacob Casler, managed to escape. The moment he discovered the enemy in ambush, and in the act of firing, he threw himself flat on the ground. After the first volley, he crawled behind a tree and waited out the passing rush of Indian warriors.

Exhilarated by their swift triumph, the inexperienced young braves and chiefs now headed straight up the road toward Colonel Cox, General Herkimer, and the 1st Battalion on the western heights. The volume of fire from the Indians and rangers on the flanks began to pick up as they closed the noose around the first three battalions of the brigade. Only Visscher's rear guard had yet to be encompassed. Joseph Brant was surveying the entire scene with a cautious eye. He and his formation of eighty would continue to crouch in concealment and wait to see what developed before launching any assault.

The militia officers, many on horseback, were prime targets for the Indian and ranger snipers and several went down in the opening volleys. One of Colonel Cox's company commanders, Capt. Jacob Dieffendorf, had just run a knife-wielding Indian through with his sword when one of his men, George Casler, called out his name to warn him of another approaching warrior. As Dieffendorf turned his head in recognition of the pronouncement of his name, he was shot dead.

General Herkimer ordered Cox to wheel his battalion into battle line to contend with the oncoming yelling Iroquois rushing down the road toward the boys of the 1st. Cox began to comply. At the first sign of the enemy, a shadow of doubt had crossed the colonel's face, but now he was bellowing orders with a frenzy. Perhaps a seed of self-recrimination had planted itself in the boastful Ebenezer's brain. If so, it was now joined by the impact of a small fiery lead sphere smashing through his temple. Cox's heavy bulk slid off his horse and crashed to the earth. The man who had maliciously insisted upon this ill-fated advance had paid the ultimate price for his vain blustering. He lay lifeless on the ground, mouth agape, and eyes wide open staring up into the heavens as though pleading.

Many militia officers were slain early on in the engagement, including Maj. Harmanus Van Slyck of the 2nd Battalion. He was one of the original twelve signatories of the Palatine District Committee of Safety's Assertion of Rights document of August 1774. He had now laid down his life in support of these measures.

According to Lt. Jacob Sammons, Lt. Abel Hunt of the 1st Battalion was also killed at about the same time as was his colonel, Ebenezer Cox. Lt. Col. William Seeber of the Canajoharie Regiment, 1st Battalion also lay mortally wounded. His last words were not about himself, but concern for his sons also fighting in the battle: "God only knows if my son Jacob lives or not, but Audolph is gone."[2]

Capt. Jacob Seeber was alive and helping General Herkimer and Maj. Samuel Campbell form the men of the 1st Battalion in preparation for the onslaught of the onrushing Iroquois warriors now heading for them up the road. Seeber formed his company in a half-circle facing the enemy on three sides. Other company commanders replicated this maneuver.

The bold frontal assault down the open road by the Indians was led by some of the newest Seneca Chiefs, just appointed at the Oswego council in July. They included Axe Carrier (Hasquesahah), Things on the Stump (Dahwahdeho), Black Feathertail (Gahnahage), Branch of a Tree (Dahgai-owned), Fish Lapper (Dahohjoedoh), and Little Billy (Jeskaka).

The brave warriors padded up the road chanting war cries, their sharp weapons uplifted in defiance. The bloodied men of the Canajoharie Regiment waited patiently for the order to commence firing as the Iroquois drew ever closer. At about one hundred paces the order was given and a solid sheet of flame erupted in the direction of the Indians.

The formation of braves was decimated. More than half of all of the Seneca chiefs and warriors to perish on this day were lost during these opening volleys, including the flower of the young leadership. Recoiling in shock, the remnants of the tattered group headed back to their main body; there to be chastised by the older Seneca chiefs, Cornplanter and Old Smoke, for their foolish tactics. The young Red Jacket, future Seneca chief and diplomat, fled back to the Genesee country with three of his companions. As this was his first war experience, nothing was ever said or done to him by the tribal elders.

The wise old chieftains explained in detail to the surviving reckless young braves the inadvisability of frontal assault across open terrain. The indirect approach was a less lethal option; sniping at the enemy from the cover of the woods and gradually wearing him down was the trick. Watching for the discharge of your adversary's musket and then rushing him before he could reload would bring success and victory this day. So the Iroquois warriors, Tory rangers, and Sir John's light infantry, ensnaring the three lead militia battalions in the fishhook formation to the west, north, and south, commenced this effective tactic. Only Visscher's 3rd Battalion had not yet tasted battle, for Joseph Brant and his contingent continued to delay entering the action against them.

With musket balls whistling by him, Brig. Gen. Nicholas Herkimer remained mounted on his white horse as a symbol of defiance to the enemy and as an extremely visible icon to his command, bolstering the morale of the men of the 1st Battalion around him who fought in the thick of it. He sent the call out to the remainder of the brigade in the eastern ravine below to move forward to the high ground to consolidate and thereby allow for a better concentration of firepower.

Klock's Palatine boys and Bellinger's Kingsland/German Flatts contingent began the advance ahead through a hail of enemy fire. They were joined by the small, yet determined band of Oneida Indians. Through this deluge of death they plunged up the road to link up with the 1st Battalion. But where was the 3rd Battalion rear guard with the ammunition wagons?

Every battle has one or more critical moments in the ebb and flow of the action. One such occasion now came for the Tryon County Militia Brigade. Anthony Van Vechten was a long time Patriot leader from the Palatine District. His loyalty to the cause was never in question. He was greatly respected by the younger men and, as a consequence, had been appointed as adjutant of Jacob Klock's 2nd Battalion. One of the primary responsibilities of the battalion adjutant is to maintain good morale, which makes it especially regrettable that Adjutant Van Vechten, at this crucial point in the engagement, simply lost his nerve.

The screams of the wounded, the stench of death, and the roar of gunfire which swirled all around him was too much for the terrified fellow. He ran back down the King's Highway, repeatedly screaming at the top of his lungs in German "Run, boys, run, or we shall all be killed!"[3] He scurried through the ranks of his own 2nd Battalion, then past the 4th's line and finally into the arms of the men of the rear guard, continually bleating his refrain.

Some of the younger lads already cowering along the roadside needed no further invitation and naturally thought this senior officer must know what he was talking about. Van Vechten carried many of them with him in the wake of his swift departure. Some officers threatened to shoot any man who joined the rout and one soldier who ignored the warning was shot by his captain.

The sight of dozens of frightened boys running scared into their midst incited a panic in many of the men of the 3rd Battalion who now joined in the headlong retreat. At subsequent court martial proceedings against the 3rd Battalion's Colonel Visscher and Lieutenant Colonel Veeder, enlisted man Henry Brath would give testimony of finding these two officers laying in a hollow in a stupefied state. During the melee when junior officers inquired if their superiors were wounded, they did not respond but stared blankly ahead, as if in shock. If they were momentarily stunned, they soon recovered with renewed vim. Visscher rode among his troops imploring them not to run like cowards; but to stand and fight like men. He rallied a good number of them and began to lead the remnants of the Mohawk Regiment back to the front to join their brigadier.

Viewing the congestion and confusion in the rear area of the militia column from his position on the southern slopes facing the supply wagons, Joseph Brant realized the optimum time to strike had arrived. He pursed the ranger's signal whistle to his lips and blew. The shrill sound floated above the din of battle taking place to the west and grabbed the attention of the already shaky rear guard and other straggling militiamen, who watched in terror as Brant's host descended whooping and firing into their midst.

At the sound of Brant's signal whistle, Col. Visscher turned his head back and watched in horror as contact with the bulk of his command was severed from his small forward party. Though he attempted to ride back and re-establish communication and a line of battle, there was no possible way to fight his way through the chaotic mass of men on the road. The routed militiamen were left to their fate. Out of approximately one hundred and ninety men, only fifty weary soldiers of the 3rd Battalion made it with their colonel to Herkimer's main body of troops grimly holding on to their weakening position along the eastern ravine and western heights.

The remainder of Visscher's rear guard was chased by the Mohawks and other Iroquois on the north flank of the fishhook for long distances to the east, down the Military Road, and through the marshy woods along Battle Creek to the north toward the Mohawk River. One by one they were run down by the fleet-footed Indians and shot, clubbed, and hacked to death. The few survivors who made there way home over the next two days were the first to inform the people of the valley settlements of the horrible ambush which had taken place near Oriska.

The main body of the militia was now completely sealed in on all sides by the Loyalists and Iroquois. The gallant Herkimer, an inspiration to his troops, continued to trot up and down the line exhorting his men. He ignored the pleas of subordinates in regards to his own personal safety. The brigadier was a veteran Indian fighter and familiar with their tactics. He encouraged his men to fan out on both flanks off the road to the north and south and seek the shelter of the fallen trees. He advised them to pair off, so that if one fired his musket and the enemy then rushed in, the second man would greet the surprised adversary with hot lead.

The now numerically superior Loyalist and Iroquois force slowly began to apply pressure on all sides, probing for weak spots. The depleted militia brigade became more compressed, but this also better focused their firepower.

The effect of Herkimer's order to push out off the road into the forest brought the Patriots into closer contact with the enemy and, as a consequence, the battle now entered a period of intense and brutal hand-to-hand combat. Former neighbors faced each other in a personal contest of blind fury.

Absent were the dressed ranks of a European battle line. There was little order—only chaos. This was a struggle between small clusters of men sandwiched between the tangled trees of a forest primeval. This was a fight of raw nerves in close quarters with the clubbed butt of a musket, the thrust of a knife or spear, or the deadly swinging of a tomahawk. Mercy would not often be requested and even more rarely be granted.

William Merckley of Stone Arabia had wandered through the woods and into the rifle sights of an Indian sharpshooter. His neighbor, Valentine Fralick of Klock's 2nd Battalion, saw him fall and came to assist him. The mortally wounded militiaman bravely waved Fralick off, murmuring

"Take care of yourself and leave me to my fate."[4] Seeing several Iroquois circling in the vicinity, Private Fralick raced a short distance away and hid himself under a fallen tree. After the Indians had passed, Valentine returned to young Merckley and found that his friend had been tomahawked and scalped. Fralick hurriedly dug a shallow grave and placed William's body into it. He then departed to seek out the main militia formation.

Pvt. Adam Miller of Colonel Visscher's 3rd Battalion was running through the underbrush when Capt. John Hare of Butler's Tory rangers popped up with a party of men and seized the frightened young boy. Col. Peter Bellinger happened to be in the area rallying his men when he witnessed the capture. Bellinger carefully aimed his pistol and squeezed the trigger. Hare fell to the forest floor in a deathly spasm. Private Miller capitalized on the opportunity to wrench himself free from the arms of his captors and ran. Later he found a discarded musket and ammunition pouch and renewed the battle against his enemies.

Earlier Col. Frederick Visscher had been unlucky to have been assigned responsibility for the supply wagons which Joseph Brant had shrewdly eyed as a primary target and subsequently overran. He now stood with the shattered remnants of his command linked with the main body of troops in the eastern ravine. The chaotic fortunes of battle now shifted in his favor as a bullet with his "name on it" whistled behind his head, grazed the back of his neck, and drew blood. A minor tilt of the head to the right or left and the colonel would have joined his fellow officer Ebenezer Cox in the hall of Valhalla. The bullet did manage to cut clean through his auburn hair, which was tied in a ribbon and hung down his back; the appendage known as a queue or "hair tail." This fashion statement of the day was retrieved and remained an honored keepsake of the Visscher family for generations.

Just as the Senecas, many of the boys of the Tryon County Militia had never participated in the rigors of mortal combat. Some, like John Duesler and Christopher Eckler of the 1st Battalion, Canajoharie Regiment, ran at the first sign of danger. They were part of Capt. Abraham Copeman's 6th Company, but in the swirling smoke and confused fighting in the dense woods they had lost sight of their officers. Disoriented, the two lads waded through a swampy region as the sounds of battle faded in the distance. Exiting out of the marshy area, they began to run and didn't stop until they found themselves along the south bank of the Mohawk River.

Ashamed, Eckler and Duesler took a couple of days to meander home. When John pushed open the door of his parent's residence, his first sight was the tear-stained countenance of his mother. Duesler's brother had also been with the militia column, had been caught in the ambush, and had been killed. Since John had also not returned with the surviving Tryon County troops, his mother had assumed that he too had perished or was a prisoner of the cruel enemy. The guilt of abandoning his brother would plague John Duesler for the remainder of his life.

George Shults, a young soldier from Stone Arabia, also ran for his life that day. In the midst of his retreat, one of the straps holding up his pants broke and his pantaloons ended up around his ankles, hampering his progress. Quickly he pulled out his hunting knife and cut himself free of the encumbrance. His shirttail flapping in the breeze, he bounded off through the woods, his white buttocks exposed for all to see. The ludicrous moment provided a brief respite from the heat of battle and brought laughter to friend and foe alike.

Capt. Jacob Seeber, whose brother Adolph was slain and whose father Lt. Col. William Seeber lay wounded and breathing his last breaths, fell with a crushed thighbone. Capt. Seeber exhibited great courage by cutting saplings and attempting to wind them about his gaping wound. One of his comrades, Henry Failing, came to him and offered to remove Seeber to a place of greater safety. The stalwart captain declined, telling Failing to load his gun with a single shot, then take the remainder of the cartridges with him, and leave the last of the Seebers to his fate. A few days later, a severely wounded Henry Failing would gaze across a crowded improvised hospital room at Fort Herkimer and witness, with heartfelt grief, the passing of Jacob Seeber.

Lt. Col. Peter Wagner, second-in-command of the Palatine Regiment, had three sons in the battle. One of them, George, was in the act of leveling his gun to fire when a bullet plowed a furrow through the fleshy part of his arm. A fellow soldier by the name of Wormuth quickly stepped forward, tore off a piece of his own shirt, and tightly wrapped it around the profusely bleeding wound. This prompt response saved George Wagner's life and cemented a life-long friendship between the two men.

Lt. Adam Quackenbush of the Mohawk Regiment experienced the intimate horror of friend versus friend in battle. He had erected the first store in Glen below present day Fultonville. He maintained a strict policy of honesty in dealing with his many Mohawk Indian patrons and they in turn had developed a healthy respect for him. When the Revolution began, many of his Mohawk friends urged Quackenbush to go to Canada with them. His love of country took precedent over his bond with the Mohawks and Adam declined. For their part, the Mohawks promised not to molest any portion of his goods or property. Along the Kings's Highway at Oriskany, Lieutenant Quackenbush faced, in regrettable fashion, many of his former native American patrons and acquaintances.

In his youth, Adam had many Mohawk playmates, who resided not far from his home. Among them was a boy named Bronkahorse, who was about the same age as Adam. They spent many carefree hours together along the banks of the Mohawk River.

At the Battle of Oriskany, the lieutenant was ducking behind trees and dodging bullets when he heard a familiar voice call his name from within gunshot range. It was his boyhood friend Bronkahorse. "Surrender yourself my prisoner," proclaimed the Mohawk warrior, "and you shall be treated kindly." "Never, will I become a prisoner!"⁵ Adam shouted back.

Each combatant warily watched for the movement of the other. Bronkahorse squeezed off the first shot; the bullet lodged in a tree scarcely an inch from Adam's head. Quackenbush crouched and, with stealth, took a new position. Raising up, Adam spotted Bronkahorse close at hand. He quickly fired, sending a musketball through his old friend's heart.

Maj. Samuel Clyde of Cherry Valley was running the fastest race of his life, leaping over logs and plunging through the brush, attempting to reach the relative safety of the main militia body. He had already lost his rifle and now ran straight into the arms of one of Butler's rangers, who knocked him down with his gun butt. The ranger was on the verge of bayoneting Samuel, when John Flock of Johnstown shot the Tory dead. Clyde enthusiastically thanked the young man, pried loose from death's grip the prize of a fine Queen Anne's musket, and rejoined his command.

Pvt. George Walter of Colonel Klock's 2nd Battalion had fallen with a severe bullet wound. Growing faint from loss of blood, he painfully crawled to a little spring and slacked his thirst. Somewhat revived, he sat up and watched the macabre carnage all around him. An Iroquois warrior lurking nearby spotted him and came sprinting over delivering a blow to the head of Walter with his tomahawk. He then proceeded to tear the scalp off the head of the helpless private.

Walter survived and years later would recall, "That Indian thought I was dead, but I knew better all the time: but I thought I would say nothing so as he would go off."⁶ Feigning death, George Walter successfully avoided any more deprivation at the hands of the enemy towering over him. He was later found by his militia comrades. Though his wounds were severe, he recovered and lived to a ripe old age, peacefully passing away fifty-four years later in August 1831.

Also in the Palatine Regiment, serving as a company commander, was Capt. Christopher W. Fox. He had been severely wounded in the right arm, yet remained in the battle with his men. They witnessed a Mohawk crawling from behind a tree toward the direction of the enemy lines. Grasping his sword in his good left hand, Fox said to his men, "You keep an eye on me for safety and I will kill an Indian."

Fox crept up and startled the warrior. A surprised look of mutual recognition crossed both men's faces. The Indian was William Johnson of Canajoharie, son of Sir William Johnson and Caroline, niece of the great Mohawk sachem Hendrick. The forlorn man was down with a shattered leg and begged for his life.

"Ah," replied the hardhearted captain, gesturing with his useless right hand, "I am wounded too, and one of us must die!"[7] The razor sharp sword silently slipped through the pleading form of William. The blood of two great Mohawk Valley families coursed through William Johnson's veins and now the precious fluid seeped into the earth of the virgin forest where once they had tread in prosperity and peace.

Captain Fox's assistant, his young nephew Peter Fox, was there in the thick of battle. As the company changed its position, Peter became oblivious to its whereabouts and wandered eastward into the enemy lines. As he was cautiously proceeding in this direction, he spied an Indian behind a tree close by, waiting for the opportunity to shoot a militiaman. The Iroquois warrior did not suspect that an adversary would be behind him. Young Fox sent a bullet through his body and he fell backward with a guttural exclamation. As he passed the fallen foe, he noted the blood running out of his mouth. Peter Fox would rejoin his uncle's company and survive the conflict.

Garret Walrath, a private in the 1st Battalion, was remembered by all who knew him as one who never feared any man, "in the flesh or the devil." Early in the engagement he was made a prisoner, pinioned, and told to keep close behind an Indian, who claimed all of his attention. Cleverly, Garret repeatedly pushed his body against his captor's, whining and complaining that his arms were too tightly drawn back. Just as often, the Iroquois brave turned around and growled at him. Unbeknown to his jailer, Walrath had a sharp hunting knife fastened in his belt. He carefully grasped the handle, watching for the right opportunity. Stumbling into his captor once again, he plunged the knife deep into the Indian's body. The liberated captive then cautiously sought his way back to his surviving companions, his bloody blade still in his hand.

Capt. Henry Diefendorf, of the town of Minden, was admirably discharging his duties as a company commander. He was suddenly shot through the lungs by a sniper, hidden under the cover of trees. Standing near him when he fell were men of his own company, William Cox and Henry Sanders. The dying man begged for water and Sanders stamped a hole in the marshy soil. As the water settled in, Henry took off his shoe and in it gave the anguished officer a drink. Cox had seen the smoke of the musket from whence the shot had come to strike down his captain. Cox uttered an oath: "Damn my soul, but I'll have a life for that one!" He ran to the tree where the enemy lay concealed. Before the Indian could reload his gun, Cox leveled his rifle straight at him. The trembling man threw up his hand imploringly shouting "You-ker! You-ker!" which Cox took to mean as a cry for mercy. "I'll give you you-ker,"⁸ stated Cox, as he sent a bullet crashing through his adversary's brain. He returned to his comrades with the Indian's musket cradled in his arms.

From the ground to a height of twenty feet, the trees were perforated with musket balls so that they "had the appearance of a building lately battered by a hailstorm." For nearly a mile along the Military Road where the militia lay trapped, the trees would take on this peculiar manifestation.

It was along the Military Road that General Herkimer now spurred his white steed back down the line from the western heights into the eastern ravine to rally his soldiers. As the brigadier plunged down the winding road, a concealed marksman took aim and let loose a blast. The bullet killed Herkimer's horse immediately and shattered the general's leg about six inches below the knee. Jacob Failing of Capt. Christian House's Company, Klock's 2nd Battalion, recalled in 1833 that he was "not over three yards from General Herkimer when he was wounded."⁹

Capt. Christopher Fox and other soldiers assisted their gravely wounded general. One of them extracted Herkimer's saddle from his prostrate horse and placed it under a birch tree. Jan Van Eps, a fourteen-year-old drummer boy from Schenectady, helped the brigadier ease into an upright position; sitting on the saddle with the tree bracing his back.

The eyes of many of his boys were focused on the general now, seeking some sign of reassurance in the midst of this horrible crisis. Though he was in great pain, Herkimer was keenly aware of the searching gazes of the wavering men. Calmly he took from his pocket a tinderbox and, with his pocket knife and a flint arrowhead, he lit his familiar pipe and continued to issue orders. With firmness and composure he spoke to his "children." Brig. Surgeon Moses Younglove, called upon to attend and dress the brigadier's wound, remembered Herkimer "exhorting his men to be valiant, telling them what amount of fame they would raise."¹⁰

Already the enemy Iroquois and rangers were trying to break through the fragile circle of men surrounding him. The militiamen retaliated by reaching out and grabbing the enemy's tomahawks and dashing out their brains with their own weapons. Subordinate officers begged the general to move to a place which would be less exposed and hazardous. Gen. Nicholas Herkimer replied by drawing his sword and thrusting the blade down into the forest ground. He then spoke loud and clear for all within listening distance to hear: "NO, I WILL FACE THE ENEMY!"[11]

His response electrified those around him and his stirring words were quickly circulated throughout the command. The Patriot militia were emboldened to make their stand. There would be no retreat. Later a speaker would liken their determined resolve to the courage of the immortal three hundred Spartans at Thermopylae, where scorning surrender, the Greeks had made a last defiant gesture on a small hilltop. Now, over two thousand years later, a brigade of American militia led by the gallant Herkimer realized they too were facing a final reckoning on a small hill and ravine in the valley of the Mohawk. The first crisis of the battle, the wounding of Herkimer, had passed. The resolve of the Patriots had solidified. The struggle was not yet one hour old.

The brave allies of the Americans, the warriors of the Oneida Indian nation, also proved their valor on this gory day. The Oneida war chief, Han Yerry Doxtater, had been shot through the right wrist, preventing him from loading his gun. He remained on horseback while his young wife, Senagena (Two Kettles Together), repeatedly loaded the musket for him. Han Yerry had a sword hanging by his side, indicative of his rank as a Patriot captain and Oneida war leader. His courageous wife stood by the chief with two pistols blazing while their son joined them in the stalwart defense. This gallant family trio would be credited with slaying eleven of the enemy. Tradition would also relate the story of the fifteen-year-old daughter of another Oneida chief being in the battle, "firing her rifle and shouting her battle cry."[12]

The Oneida warrior Blatcop would particularly distinguish himself in combat. Three times he engaged in a hand-to-hand melee, fighting with his tomahawk, swinging it with deadly force to the right and left. An eye witness account had Blatcop breaking the arm of an Indian Loyalist with one powerful swoop.

Louis, a St. Regis Indian residing with the Oneidas, was agitated. When asked what was the matter, he replied, "There is one of the black serpents lying in the fork of a fallen tree, and every time he rises up he kills one of our men. I can stand it no longer—either he or I must die." With these words he raised his rifle and fired. The opposing Indian leapt up into the air and fell dead across the fork of the tree which had sheltered him. Louis gave out a wild whoop, then ran up to his victim, tearing off the dead man's scalp. He then returned to his friends, throwing the bloody trophy on the ground before them and said, "That fellow will do no more harm."

Thomas Spencer, the Oneida's blacksmith who had forewarned the militia of the approach of St. Leger's move against Fort Stanwix, was in the thick of the action. Today he would give his life for the Patriot cause. In the midst of the fray, Thomas found himself confronted by an old Mohawk neighbor. Each man drew his knife, but the Mohawk found his mark first.

The Oneida Indian Nation was America's first ally in war. They had proven themselves worthy in their first engagement of the War of Independence, the Battle of Oriskany.

The ambush had begun one hour earlier and finally a tolerable order had been established in the militia's ranks; but the superior enemy force was closing in on all sides. It was at this juncture that divine providence interceded in the form of a heavy rain shower, stopping most of the firing for the better part of another hour. Herkimer's soldiers were able to organize more perfectly; to consolidate and strengthen the beleaguered formation. Orders were issued once again to place two men behind each tree with instructions for only one man to fire his musket at a time. This would counteract the tactics of the Iroquois, who whenever they saw a musket discharged from behind a tree, would run up and tomahawk its owner before he had time to reload.

During the storm the combatants sought shelter as best they could. Pvt. John Petrie of Bellinger's 4th Battalion concealed himself under the cover of a large tree. Soon after, he heard a whooping sound and, looking in the direction of the noise, saw several enemy Indians coming together within gunshot range. He drew up his piece and brought down a large warrior, much to the surprise of the war party who were puzzled that anyone had been able to keep their powder dry during the torrential downpour. The rain prevented them from seeing the smoke of the musket barrel to determine where the bullet that laid out their comrade had come from. They took the precaution of changing their position, but when they heard the ominous click of Petrie's gun once again, they fled into the depths of the woods.

By noon the rain had subsided and the fight was resumed with deadly ardor. It was now that Sir John Johnson, who had up to this point allowed the Iroquois and rangers do the bulk of the fighting and dying, dispatched onto this field of glory a contingent of the Loyalist King's Royal Regiment of New York.

Who were these colonists of Scottish and Irish descent who advanced so resolutely against the Patriots in their crisp green uniforms, with bayonets fixed, during this pivotal moment in the battle? The ancestors of Sir John and the King's Royal Regiment had struggled for freedom in Ireland and Scotland during the long Jacobite Rebellion from 1690 until the mid 1700's.

In 1690, James II landed in Ireland and faced the English King, William III, on the banks of the River Boyne in an attempt to reclaim his throne. Serving as an officer in King James' own regiment was Sir John Johnson's great grandfather Warren. At the Battle of Boyne old Ireland finally "collapsed under the English conqueror's heel."[13] It was along the banks of the Mohawk River that Warren's descendants and the families of other Irish rebels found sanctuary in the New World.

In 1746, the hopes of Scottish independence were dashed at the brief and bloody engagement on a rain soaked hillside near Inverness at Culloden Moor. The Johnson family welcomed the defeated but unbowed Scots to their fertile fields in the valley.

Today, the sons and grandsons of these freedom loving expatriates were advancing shoulder to shoulder across another storm-drenched slope with grim determination against their former Palatine neighbors. They had grown up imbued with the bitter wine of exile from their native Ireland and Scotland. They did not wish their children to inherit the same legacy as refugees.

The sight of the green coats of the Tryon County Loyalists, who had so harassed the Patriots in the valley during their brief regime at the beginning of the Revolution, brought a fever pitch of emotion to the surface on the militia side. The Loyalists, too, had vengeance on their minds, for they had been unceremoniously evicted from their hearths and homes in the Mohawk Valley by the rebels.

The steady ranks of the militia fired once upon the king's men, but did not wait under the shelter of the trees to deliver a second volley. Herkimer's boys rushed out to meet the bristling line of Johnson's Greens with bayonets, clubbed muskets, and hunting knives in a wild melee which lasted for almost half an hour. Capt. Andrew Dillenbeck of the Palatine Regiment was assailed by three Loyalist soldiers; he brained one, shot the second, and bayoneted the third before he succumbed and perished. Capt. Jacob Gardinier of Visscher's 3rd Battalion would be wounded an incredible thirteen times during the onslaught. Even then, as he stood bleeding, he managed to stab three Tories with his spear.

It was now about one o'clock in the afternoon. Above the din of battle, from the direction of Fort Stanwix three hours after the ambush had begun, the sweet sound of three cannon was heard booming in succession. Finally, the signal had been issued by Gansevoort. This caused the battered militia to be reinvigorated with the faint hope of relief on the way. The Iroquois Loyalists also took notice.

Seeing a break in the battle beginning to take shape, Col. John Butler offered a suggestion. Perhaps a ruse could be undertaken. If the militia expected reinforcements, why not provide them with the same in the form of our own men in disguise? It was agreed to by Sir John Johnson. Sir John's brother-in-law, Maj. Stephen Watts, a popular figure with the men, led a fresh detachment of Loyalists onto the field with their green coats turned inside out. From a distance they appeared to be soldiers from Fort Stanwix.

As the Tories neared the militia line, Capt. Jacob Gardinier was not fooled. With a few of his men, he waded into the midst of the enemy, killed one of their officers, Captain McDonald, and held his corpse by the collar as a shield against the bullets and bayonets of the enemy. Finally, riddled through with bayonet and bullet wounds, the courageous Gardinier crept into a cavity at the roots of a fallen tree where he continued the fight aided by a young German lad. The boy would venture out periodically and bring Jacob the guns of the fallen, loading those requiring it, which the captain gamely used to the detriment of the enemy.

In a work published after the war by the Reverend Johan Daniel Gros, it was stated: "Let it stand recorded among other patriotic deeds of that little army of militia, that a Jacob Gardinier, with a few of his men, vanquished a whole platoon."[14]

During this desperate charge an officer of the King's Royal Regiment of New York, Stephen Watts, had been gravely wounded; Pvt. Henry Failing of the Canajoharie Regiment had stumbled upon him. In one of the few gestures of kindness uncovered during this hellish contest, Failing carried the seriously injured Watts to a tiny stream of water that he might drink and ease his thirst and smooth his passage into the next world. A grateful Watts handed the private his gold pocketwatch with gracious thanks and wished him Godspeed. For two days the unfortunate Watts would languish on the battlefield, with only wolves for company in the twilight hours, until he was discovered by some friendly Iroquois.

It was now 2:00 P.M., August 6, 1777. The sounds of gunfire could be heard coming from the British camp to the west. With this disturbing sound, the Iroquois added concern to the rage they already felt for the terrible losses they had suffered. The flower of their young leadership lay stiff and cold on the ground of this wilderness inferno of death. Their hearts were no longer in this fight. The old chiefs were bitter at the thought of what had been promised by the British at the Oswego Council a few weeks before. They were supposed to have been only spectators at this encounter, not bloodied participants.

Capt. John James Davis had made a miraculous journey in the last four hours. As part of Visscher's rear guard, he had successfully fought his way up to the main body and survived the ferocious onslaught of Johnson's Greens. He cocked his head and listened to the musketry drifting down from the vicinity of Fort Stanwix with a contented look on his face. He also took note of the lull that had begun to descend onto the battlefield. Ens. Richard Putnam commented hopefully to the captain, "I believe the red devils have pretty much all left us." To which Davis replied, "They are not all gone, some of them are lurking about here yet."[15] Scarcely had these words passed his lips when a musket ball punctured the throat of the prophetic Captain Davis, who fell with a gurgle and expired. He was perhaps the last casualty on the field this day. Seven hundred and sixty soldiers of the Tryon County Militia and sixty warriors of the Oneida Indian Nation had entered this bloody ravine. Now barely one hundred and fifty were left standing on the western heights and the tip of the eastern gully. The wounded General Herkimer reclined near the center of this ragged circle drifting in and out of consciousness.

"Oonah... Oonah..."[15] the Iroquois call for retreat drifted across the battlefield. There were far fewer braves to answer the call than there had been five hours before. Soon the Indians and Tory rangers were joined in their gradual exit to the west by the tattered remains of the King's Royal Regiment of New York, led by a stunned Sir John Johnson. Survivors on both sides were treated to one last macabre spectacle symbolic of the horror of the conflict. Sometime during the battle, one of Herkimer's men had been pinned to a tree with a bayonet and suspended several feet off the ground. The body would remain in this position until its own decomposition caused the cadaver to slump to the ground. For more than a quarter of a century the bayonet could still be seen where it had been driven into the tree, a fitting memorial to the savagery of the struggle.

It was three o'clock in the afternoon, August 6, 1777. The Battle of Oriskany was over.

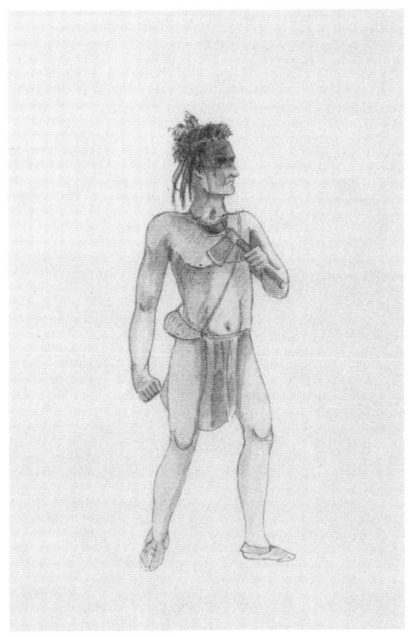

Warrior of the Mohawk Indian Nation. Illustration by David Yahnke

Tory ranger officer, illustration by David Yahnke

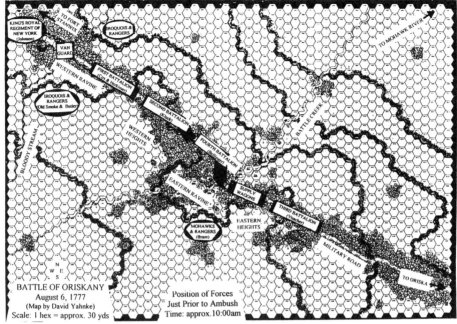

KING'S ROYAL REGIMENT OF NEW YORK (Johnson)

TO FORT STANWIX

IROQUOIS & RANGERS

VAN GUARD

WESTERN RAVINE

FIRST BATTALION (Cox & Hess...)

TO MOHAWK RIVER

IROQUOIS & RANGERS (Old Smoke & Butler)

SECOND BATTALION (Klock)

WESTERN HEIGHTS

FOURTH BATTALION

BATTLE CREEK

BLOODY STREAM

EASTERN RAVINE

SUPPLY WAGONS

THIRD BATTALION (Visscher)

MOHAWKS & RANGERS (Brant)

EASTERN HEIGHTS

MILITARY ROAD

TO ORISKA

N
W   E
S

BATTLE OF ORISKANY
August 6, 1777
(Map by David Yahnke)
Scale: 1 hex = approx. 30 yds

Position of Forces
Just Prior to Ambush
Time: approx. 10:00am

Author's collection

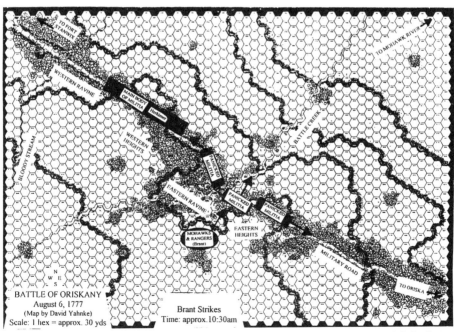

TO FORT STANWIX

TO MOHAWK RIVER

WESTERN RAVINE

MAIN BODY OF MILITIA   Herkimer

WESTERN HEIGHTS

BATTLE CREEK

BLOODY STREAM

PANICKED MILITIA

EASTERN RAVINE

PANICKED MILITIA

PANICKED MILITIA

MOHAWKS & RANGERS (Brant)

EASTERN HEIGHTS

MILITARY ROAD

TO ORISKA

N
W   E
S

BATTLE OF ORISKANY
August 6, 1777
(Map by David Yahnke)
Scale: 1 hex = approx. 30 yds

Brant Strikes
Time: approx. 10:30am

Author's collection

THE BATTLE-GROUND OF ORISKANY.[1]

The Oriskany Battlefield in 1848, from Lossing's *Pictorial Field Book of the Revolution*, collection of the Oneida County Historical Society

"Leave me to my fate," enactment, collection of James Morrison

Men of the First Battalion let loose a volley, enactment, collection of James Morrison

"I will face the enemy. . .", illustration by David Yahnke

"Two men behind every tree. . .", illustration by David Yahnke

Soldier of the King's Royal Regiment of New York, illlustration by David Yahnke

Warrior of the Oneida Indian Nation, illustration by David Yahnke

On Fame's eternal camping ground
Their silent tents are spread
And Glory guards, with solemn round,
The bivouac of the dead.
—*Theodore O'Hara*

Chapter Eight

AFTERMATH

Photo by the author

The death bed of Nicholas Herkimer, an enactment, courtesy of the New York State Office of Parks, Recreation, and Historic Preservation, Herkimer Home State Historic Site

The battle on the field had ceased, but for the men of the Tryon County Militia taken prisoner by the Loyalists and Iroquois, their cruel ordeal was just beginning.

Henry Walrath had fought with the main body of the small army as a member of John Hess' company in Klock's battalion, and had been engaged in the hottest part of the action. Three of his companions were shot down by his side. Walrath fired nine times and then the Indians rushed up and took him captive. The warriors tied a rope around his neck and fastened him to a tree. When the Iroquois withdrew from the vicinity, the twelve of them brought the unlucky Henry along with their other plunder from the supply carts.

The Indians dragged Walrath into the British camp, proudly displaying their prize to Barry St. Leger. The English commander inquired of Walrath as to his appetite and offered him some victuals. The warriors then took the militia captive to their own camp about a half mile distant. This was the initiation of a perilous journey for young Walrath, which took him to Quebec, then by stormy seas to New York City. Finally during the bitter winter of 1777-78, he was transported by sleigh to Albany where he was released in January 1778 as part of a parole exchange.

John Spanable had also been marching with Jacob Klock to link up with General Herkimer and the 1st Battalion when they had unexpectedly encountered a party of enemy Indians. Spanable was captured and taken to Canada. One night as they laid in their blankets, the Iroquois began howling, lamenting the loss of their comrades at Oriskany. Spanable understood their dialect. The Indians' mourning also brought to the militiaman's mind his many good friends slain on that bloody field. He began to cry out in a similar fashion to his captors.

The enemy supposed Spanable was being sympathetic to their own plight and treated him with marked kindness for the rest of the journey. When they arrived at the Indian camp, he was exempted from "running the gauntlet," a terrible ordeal which other prisoners were made to suffer. Spanable survived his long imprisonment to die of old age in Stone Arabia.

The reader may recall the mention of Robert Crouse from Fort Plain, who had so impressed Gen. Philip Schuyler the previous winter with his feats of strength. Crouse was now the prisoner of a sadistic enemy. The vengeful Indians murdered at least a dozen of their captives and tortured to death a half dozen more. Robert Crouse was one of them. His enormous stature, six and a half feet in his boots, gave them the grotesque idea of "cutting him down to size."[1] With their knives, they amputated his legs at the knee joints. Jeering, they held up the bloody limbs and informed Crouse he now stood as tall as everyone else and bade him to walk. As the

Patriot lay in agony, they shortened his suffering by dispatching him with their knives and tearing off his scalp.

Toward the end of the battle, Brig. Surgeon Moses Younglove had surrendered himself a prisoner to an Iroquois warrior. The Indian gave him up to a sergeant of Sir John's regiment. A Tory ranger by the name of Lieutenant Ginnis strode up with other Loyalists, pushing himself into Younglove's face with the fire of hate in his eyes. The Tory drew his tomahawk and was barely persuaded to spare the doctor's life. The lieutenant took Younglove's watch, buckles, spurs, and other personal items. Other Loyalists, following Ginnis[1] example, stripped the prisoner almost naked. All around Younglove fellow captives were being similarly tormented and then butchered as the doctor watched in horror and outrage.

Younglove was dragged before Col. John Butler, who demanded of him what he was fighting for. The surgeon replied that he "fought for the liberty that God and nature gave him and to defend himself and his dearest connections from the massacre of the savages." Butler replied, "You are a damned, impudent rebel,"[2] and he then encouraged his subordinates to kill this stubborn prisoner and other captives who were there.

Lieutenant Singleton of Johnson's command had been seriously wounded and was particularly vehement in encouraging the slaughter. Younglove survived this beating only to experience the depravity of slow starvation. When provisions were made available, they were of the worst kind, such as spoiled flour and moldy biscuits full of maggots. The torture and murder of prisoners became a daily ritual in camp.

At the fore of the King's Royal Regiment of New York, Sir John Johnson, Baronet, rode westward in stunned silence, numb to the lamentations of the militia captives. He had envisioned a triumphant return to his beloved Johnstown parading through the streets at the head of an impressive military formation, the laurel crown of victory perched above his brow as the assembled masses cheered themselves hoarse.

Instead, he had served as the angel of death descending amidst the huddled forms of the valley inhabitants. As he paused at a brook to wash the blood of the innocent from his hands, Sir John was struck by the revelation that this was what came with empire building. He had not asked for this. Sir John simply wanted to come home to the comfort and tranquility of Johnson Hall.

Deep in his heart John Johnson realized this would not have been his father's way. Sir William could never have brought himself to lift his hand in violence against his neighbors. The clever and resourceful old sod undoubtedly would have crafted a diplomatic solution to the issue, preserving his interests while at the same time satisfying the libertarian yearnings of the valley Whigs. His mortified son keenly felt the pain of his absence on this apocalyptic day.

Back on the battlefield Capt. Christopher W. Fox, sword in hand, was surveying the carnage that surrounded him. As far as the eye could see was strewn the debris of war; discarded weapons and equipment, the wounded, the dying, the dead. He witnessed one of the youths of his command, stumbling over the wreckage of conflict, going from one man to another repeating the same question: "Have you seen my brother? Have you seen my brother?"[3]

Captain Fox took the boy by the arm and together they journeyed across the war torn terrain until they came to a small hill. There on the slopes a number of bodies lay slumped together face down in the soil. One by one they turned the corpses over. They had all been scalped and their faces had been disfigured to such a degree as to render them almost unrecognizable. As they rolled over one of the forms, a shocked expression came across the youth's face and he went off muttering: "I have no more brother. I have no more brother."[4]

The Battle of Oriskany was the bloodiest engagement of the American Revolution and perhaps, if the percentage of casualties is considered, of any battle in U.S. history. On the sixth of August 1777, between the hours of 10 A.M. and 3 P.M., the Tryon County Militia Brigade lost a total of approximately four hundred fifty men killed, wounded, and captured out of seven hundred sixty engaged. A stunning fifty-nine percent of the formation had been lost. Ironically, fewer men were lost as a percentage at George Custer's Battle of Little Big Horn, yet that battle captured the imagination of the American public one hundred years later.

At least four members of the original Tryon County Committee of Safety had been slain, including Samuel Billington, John Dygert, Isaac Paris, and Jacob Snell. Six other members of the Snell family were also dead or wounded on the field. Paris had been captured, beaten, and murdered by an enemy who knew him intimately.

The Iroquois and Loyalists had suffered heavy losses as well, though not at the same magnitude as the Patriots. Perhaps two hundred were killed, wounded, or missing out of seven hundred engaged.

The Seneca warriors in particular had suffered greatly. Five of their young chiefs were dead: Axe Carrier, Things on the Stump, Black Feathertail, Branch of a Tree, and Fish Lapper. Thirty Seneca braves had also been slain and almost an equal number were hobbled by wounds. By Iroquois standards, these were terrible losses. This had not been their style of warfare. A five-hour, set-piece struggle was not the Iroquois tradition of waging war. Swift, decisive actions with a minimum sacrifice of human life by both sides was more common. The Iroquois who were allied with the Loyalists were largely demoralized by the unholy butchering which had taken place.

The Patriots were masters of the field but incapable of moving westward to the relief of Fort Stanwix. It was enough that the survivors summoned the strength to gather the wounded onto makeshift litters. The dead were abandoned where they had fallen. Time was of the essence, for the prospect loomed that a reinforced adversary would return to the slaughter.

The shattered remnants of the gallant Tryon County Militia Brigade which had so resolutely set out at dawn that morning began the mournful journey home to the valley with their wounded brigadier barely conscious. When they arrived, the entire community would be wracked with grief, for hardly a family remained that had not left a father, son, or brother in that wooded tomb.

Years later, militiaman John Lewis would recall that at the village of Oriska, a carriage was secured to transport the gravely injured General Herkimer to his estate on the south bank of the Mohawk River, a couple of miles below Little Falls. Part of his journey would be by boat. Asst. Brig. Surgeon Dr. Petry, although himself seriously wounded, had done his best to dress the general's shattered leg on the field and saw him placed on a litter. At the time, he did not consider Herkimer's wound to be fatal.

In the absence of Petry and the captured Dr. Younglove, a young doctor would attend to Nicholas Herkimer in his home. Robert Johnston had accompanied Gen. Benedict Arnold's relief column as it marched up the Mohawk Valley in an attempt to break the siege at Fort Stanwix. The youthful physician was now entrusted with the care of the beloved leader of the valley Patriots. On the morning of August 16, 1777, the inexperienced Dr. Johnston wrongly decided to amputate General Herkimer's injured leg. The arteries were not properly sealed and all through the night the brigadier's wound bled profusely.

By evening when the error was discovered, the general was extremely weak. With his faithful wife Maria by his side, he whispered for the family Bible. This book of holy scripture, written in German, had made the epic trip across the ocean with Nicholas' grandparents from the Palatinate those many years before. Now in the gathering darkness the words would comfort the native son in his moment of agony. Herkimer, distraught because of his physical pain and the belief that he had failed his "children," would never know of the events unfolding in the Mohawk Valley in 1777 as he lay dying. The general's fingers painfully turned the frayed parchment until his eyes rested prophetically on the words of Psalm 38 and in a hoarse murmur he began to recite it:

Psalm 38, Verse 1

O Lord, rebuke me not in thy wrath: nor chasten me in thy hot displeasure.

August 6, 1777

To The Defenders of Fort Stanwix,

Soldiers, you have heard that General Herkimer is on his march to our relief. The commanding officer feels satisfied that the Tories and the Queen's Rangers have stolen off in the night with Brant and his Mohawks, to meet him. The camp of Sir John Johnson is therefore weakened. As many of you as feel willing to follow me in an attack upon it, and not afraid to die for liberty, will shoulder your arms, and step out one pace to the front.

—Marinus Willett, Second in Command, Ft. Stanwix

Lt. Col., 3rd NY Continental Regiment[5]

Verse 2

For thine arrows stick fast in me, and thy hand presseth me sore.

August 7

At 11 o'clock this evening, the enemy came near the fort, called to our sentinels, telling them to come out again with fixed bayonets and they would give satisfaction for yesterday's work.

—From the Journal of William Colbrath, soldier

Fort Stanwix Garrison

Verse 3

There is no soundness in my flesh because of thine anger; neither is there any rest in my bones because of my sin.

August 7

To Peter Gansevoort,

It is with concern we are to acquaint you that this was the fatal day in which the succors, which were intended for your relief, have been attacked and defeated, with great loss of numbers killed, wounded and taken prisoners. Our regard for your safety and lives, and our sincere advice to you is, if you will avoid inevitable ruin and destruction, to surrender the fort you pretend to defend against a formidable body of troops.

—Frederick Bellinger and John Frey

Captured Officers of the Tryon County Militia[6]

Verse 4

For mine iniquities are gone over my head: as a heavy burden they are too heavy for me.

August 8

Verbally delivered to Peter Gansevoort,

I am directed by Colonel St. Leger to inform the commandant, that the colonel has, with much difficulty, prevailed on the Indians to agree, that if the garrison, without further resistance, shall be delivered up to the investing army, the officers and soldiers shall have all their baggage and personal property secured to them... Colonel Butler accompanies me to assure them, that not a hair of the head of any one of them shall be hurt..

Should the present terms be rejected, it will be out of the power of the colonel to restrain the Indians ... from plundering the property and destroying the lives of the greater part of the garrison... the colonel will not be able to prevent them from marching down the country and destroying the settlements with their inhabitants...

—British Major Ancrum[7]

With Gansevoort's permission, Marinus Willett replies,

... You have made a long speech on the occasion of your visit, which, stripped of its superfluities, amounts to this... to tell the commandant that if he does not deliver up the garrison into the hands of your colonel, he will send his Indians to murder our women and children... I consider the message you have brought a degrading one for a British officer to send... For my part, I declare, before I would consent to deliver this garrison to such a murdering set as your army, I would suffer my body to be filled with splinters and set on fire...

Marinus Willett,
Patriot[8]

Verse 5

My wounds stink and are corrupt because of my foolishness.

August 9

Peter Gansevoort replies to St. Leger's written demand for surrender, ... It is my determined resolution, with the forces under my command to defend this fort and garrison to the last extremity, in behalf of the United American States, who have placed me here to defend it against all their enemies.[9]

Verse 6

I am troubled; I am bowed down greatly; I go mourning all the day long.

August 9

To the Albany County Committee of Safety,

... The flower of our militia either killed or wounded, except 150, who stood the field and forced the enemy to retreat; the wounded were brought off by these brave men...

—Peter Dygert
Surviving member of Tryon County Committee of Safety[10]

Verse 7

My loins are filled with a loathsome disease: and there is no soundness in my flesh.

> *August 11*
>
> *To Governor George Clinton,*
>
> *...The Troops have done their duty, and the Militia have behaved very brave, General Herkimer merits the greatest praise; he after having his thigh broke, sat on a log with a drawn sword inspiring his men, for several hours; he was repeatedly solicited by his friends to be carried from the field of action, which he absolutely refused. We can assure you that at the same time, our warmest advocates and bravest friends of Tryon County fell in that skirmish. They are dispirited and call for help...*
>
> —Albany County Committee of Safety[11]

Verse 8

I am feeble and sore broken: I have roared by reason of the disquietness of my heart.

> *August 11*
>
> *This day the enemy having observed that we brought water from the creek, altered its course so that it became dry. This would have done us much damage had we not been able to open two wells in the garrison...*
>
> —From the Journal of William Colbrath[12]

Verse 9

Lord, all my desire is before thee; and my groaning is not hid from thee.

> *August 13*
>
> *To the Inhabitants of Tryon County,*
>
> *Notwithstanding the many and great injuries we have received in person and property at your hands, and being at the head of victorious troops, we most ardently wish to have peace restored to this once happy country... You have, no doubt, great reason to dread the resentment of the Indians, on account of the loss they sustained in the late action... Surrounded as you are by victorious armies... without any resource, surely you can not hesitate a moment to accept the terms proposed to you by friends and well wishers...*
>
> —John Johnson, Daniel Claus, and John Butler
> Loyalist leaders[13]

Verse 10

My heart panteth, my strength faileth me: as the light of mine eyes, it is also gone from me

> *August 14*
>
> *Toward evening they were again at their old play, cannonading and bom-*

barding us. A shell bursting slightly wounded one of Colonel Mellon's men in the head. No other damage was done...

—From the Journal of William Colbrath[14]

Verse 11

My lovers and my friends stand aloof from my sore; and my kinsmen stand afar off.

August 15

I think it my duty in our present situation to guard as much as possible against the disgrace of a surprise; therefore order all troops belonging to this garrison to turn out to their alarm posts at 2 o'clock every morning...

—From the Orderly Book of Peter Gansevoort
Commandant, Fort Stanwix[15]

Verse 12

They also that seek after my life lay snares for me: and they that seek my hurt speak mischievous things, and imagine deceits all the day long.

August 15

To Sir Guy Carleton,

...We heard the rebels in full march with a convoy of 15 wagons... We were immediately formed by the Seneca Chiefs, who took the lead in this action, in concurrence with Sir John and myself... During the whole action the Indians showed the greatest zeal for his Majesty's cause and had they not been a little too precipitate, scarcely a rebel of the party would have escaped....

—John Butler[16]

Verse 13

But I, as a deaf man, heard not; and I was as a dumb man that openeth not his mouth.

August 16

A party of our men were ordered out this evening to bring in wood for the garrison, and being discovered by some skulking Indians, gave the alarm to the rest. They advanced near where our men were at work, but luckily our men had been called in before they became nigh enough to do any mischief...

—From the Journal of William Colbrath[17]

Verse 14

Thus I was as a man that heareth not, and in whose mouth are no reproofs.

August 16

To General George Washington

I am just informed that Lt. Col. Willett is arrived at Albany. He found the militia of Tryon County collecting with great alacrity and as General Arnold with the troops marched under his command will probably reach German Flatts on the 16th or 17th.

—Philip Schuyler
Patriot General Commanding Northern Department[18]

Verse 15
For in thee, 0 Lord, do I hope: thou wilt hear, O Lord my God.
August 17
To Dr. Potts, Director of the General Hospital for the Northern Department, Yesterday morning I amputated General Herkimer's leg, there not being left the prospect of recovery without it. But alas, the patriotic hero died in the evening—the cause of his death God only knows... Nothing more surprised me, but we cannot always parry death, so there is an end to it...

—Robert Johnston
Attending physician[19]

August 18
The advance guard to keep double sentinels every night until further orders.
—From the Orderly Book of Peter Gansevoort[20]

August 18
To the Inhabitants of Tryon County,
Whereas, a certain Barry St. Leger.. at the head of a banditti of robbers, murderers and traitors... have lately appeared on the frontiers of this state, and have threatened ruin and destruction to all inhabitants of the United States... Humanity to these poor deluded wretches, who are hastening blindfold to destruction, induces me to offer them pardon, provided they do within ten days from the date hereof come and lay down their arms... But if still blind to their own safety, they obstinately persist in their wicked courses... they must expect no mercy...

—Benedict Arnold,
Major General, Continental Army[21]

Convicted as a spy at the same time as Walter Butler was Han Yost Schuyler, reputed to be a half-wit, yet in some respects shrewd. He was regarded by the Indians with the respect and reverence which they customarily paid to fools and lunatics. At the pleading of Schuyler's family, General Arnold agreed that Han Yost could escape execution if he would go at once to St. Leger's camp and exaggerate the size of Arnold's relief column now approaching Fort Stanwix. Before setting off, Schuyler removed his coat and had several shots fired through it to substantiate his tale of escape.

August 20

To General Philip Schuyler,

I leave this place this morning with twelve hundred Continental troops and a handful of militia for Fort Stanwix, which is still besieged by a number equal to ours... You will hear of my being victorious or no more, and as soon as the safety of this part of the country will permit I will fly to your assistance.

—Benedict Arnold
Major General[22]

August 22

This afternoon the Honorable Major General Arnold arrived here with near 1,000 men. They were saluted with a discharge of powder from our mortars and all the cannon from bastion... attended with three cheers from the troops...

—From the Journal of William Colbrath[23]

August 23

The General returns his thanks to Col. Gansevoort, the officers and soldiers under his command for their gallant defense of Fort Stanwix... They may be assured of his warmest recommendations to Congress...

—Benedict Arnold
Major General[24]

August 27

To General Burgoyne

The same zeal no longer animated the Indians; they complained of the thinness of our troops and their former losses ... When upon the ground appointed for the field of battle, scouts came in with an account... that General Burgoyne's army was cut to pieces, and that Arnold was advancing by rapid and forced marches with 3,000 men. It was at this moment that I began to suspect cowardice in some and treason in others.... A council according their custom was called... before the breaking up which I learned that 200 were already decamped In about an hour they insisted that I should retreat or they would be obliged to abandon me. I had no other party to take, and a hard party it was to troops who could do nothing without them... and therefore proposed to retire at night, sending on my sick, wounded and artillery down the Wood Creek, covering them by our line of march....

—Lt. Col. St. Leger[25]

August 28

An Indian Chief with three other Indians arrived in camp from Lt. Col. St.

Leger, who upon receiving certain intelligence of the approach of an army of 3,000 men, commanded by Mr. Arnold, and suspecting cowardice in some of his savages and treason in others, had raised the siege of Fort Stanwix, and retreated to Oswego.

—From the Journal of an Officer of the British 47th Regiment of Foot[26]

November 6
To British Secretary of War Knox, The Indian action near Fort Stanwix, happening near a settlement of Oneida Indians in the rebel's interest, who were at the same time in arms against our party, the Six Nations Indians, after the action, burnt their houses, destroyed their field crops and killed and carried away their cattle. This the rebel Oneidas, after our retreat, revenged upon Joseph's sister and her family, robbing them of cash, clothes and cattle, and driving them from their home; then proceeding to the Mohawk's town and dealt in the same manner with the poor women and children whose husbands were in the King's service. Joseph's sister and family fled to Onondaga, the council place of the Six Nations with whom she had always had a great sway during the late Sir William Johnson's lifetime, and even now....

—Daniel Claus[27]

On May 28, 1778, Colonel Frederick Visscher was charged with cowardice as a result of the conduct of the rear guard at Oriskany.
On June 16, the Council of Appointments presented their findings:
RESOLVED therefore that the consideration of the said complaints be
    postponed and the Council...as they esteem for the good of their Country, they forbear from any further disputes that may tend to disunite the Inhabitants of Tryon County and heartily to assist each other in the most vigorous exertions to repel the common enemy...

In June of 1782, General George Washington was dining in Schenectady and requested the attendance of Colonel Visscher. Dinner was not served until Visscher arrived and the slandered officer was seated in a place of honor at Washington's right hand.

September 1778
At the first onset the Senecas lost 17 men among whom were several Chiefs and leaders which enraged them greatly and although the rebels were put to flight and left upwards of 500 killed on the spot, yet that was not sufficient satisfaction and their principal Chief, Old Smoke, a descendant of a brave and loyal family who were distinguished for their loyalty and attachment to the British interest so early in the reign of Queen Anne and were presented by the Queen with a coronet. The only mark of distinction of that kind ever given to

any of the Six Nations. This brave Seneca Chief, asking for a small body of white men to join the Indians and Mr. Brant proposed to Sir John and Col. Claus to pursue the blow and Sir John mentioned it to Lt. Colonel St. Leger. But the Lt. Colonel gave his reasons why he could not approve of it and the matter was dropped. Not long after upon false alarms the siege was raised and the army retreated to Oswego to join Gen. Burgoyne by the way of Canada....

—Daniel Claus
From his papers[28]

In October of 1777, the Continental Congress directed that a monument should be erected to the memory of Brig. Gen. Nicholas Herkimer, of the value of five hundred dollars. A letter accompanying the resolution read:

"Every mark of distinction shown to the memory of such illustrious men as offer up their lives for the liberty and happiness of this country, reflects real honor on those who pay the grateful tribute; and by holding up to others the prospect of fame and immortality, will animate them to tread in the same path."

Governor George Clinton forwarded the letter and resolution to the Tryon County Committee, adding: "We regret to state that no monument has ever been erected to his memory in pursuance of that or any other resolve."

Burgoyne attired himself in full court dress and wore costly regimentals and a richly decorated hat with streaming plumes. Gates, a smaller man, on the contrary was dressed merely in a plain blue overcoat. Upon the two generals first catching a glimpse of each other, they stepped forward simultaneously and advanced, until they were only a few steps apart, when they halted. The English general took off his hat, and making a polite bow, said, "The fortunes of war, General Gates, has made me your prisoner."[29]

Sunday April 20, 1783
...I then proceeded for Oriska Creek and between the summit of the hill and the creek, I went over the ground where General Herkimer fought Sir John Johnson. This allowed likewise to one of the most desperate struggles that has ever been fought by the militia. I saw a vast number of human skulls and bones scattered through the woods....

—Diary of Lt. Alexander Thompson
2nd Artillery, Continental Army[30]

"I have no more brother . . .", illustration by David Yahnke

The journey home, illustration by David Yahnke

"Aftermath," illustration by David Yahnke

Corporal, drum sergeant major, and wagoneer of the Fort Stanwix garrison at enactment, courtesy of the National Park Service, Fort Stanwix National Monument

"Cannonading and bombarding us . . .", at enactment, courtesy of National Park Service, Fort Stanwix National Monument

Burgoyne's surrender to Gates, from Lee's *Pictorial History of the American Revolution*, collection of the Oneida County Historical Society

"Death of a Patriot," illustration by David Yahnke

HERKIMER'S GRAVE

Grave of the forgotten hero in the early 1800's, from Cowen's *The Herkimers and Schuylers*, collection of the Oneida County Historical Society

Appendix I

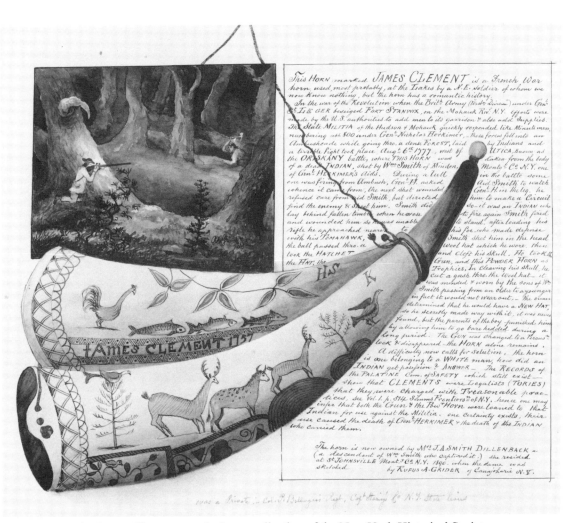

The James Clement powder horn, collection of the New York Historical Society

THE MAN WHO SHOT GENERAL HERKIMER

This horn marked JAMES CLEMENT is a French War horn used, most probably, at the Lakes by a N.E. Soldier of whom we know nothing, but the horn has a romantic history.

In the war of the Revolution when the British Army (Western Division) under General St. LEGER besieged FORT STANWIX on the Mohawk River N.Y., efforts were made by the U.S. authorities to add men to its garrison & also add supplies. The State MILITIA of the Hudson and Mohawk quickly responded like Minute men, numbering about 800 under General Nicholas Herkimer—those forces fell into an Ambuscade while going through a dense FOREST, laid by Indians and a terrible fight took place August 6th, 1777, west of UTICA, known as the ORISKANY battle, where THIS HORN was taken from a body of a dead INDIAN, shot by William Smith of Minden, Montgomery County, N.Y. one of General HERKIMER'S Aides. During a lull in the battle some one was firing from Ambush, General Herkimer asked Aide Smith to watch whence it came from, the next shot wounded General Herkimer in the leg, he refused care from Aide Smith, but directed him to make a circuit find the enemy & shoot him. Smith did so—it was an INDIAN who lay behind fallen timbers, when he arose to fire again Smith fired and wounded him so he was unable to stand, after loading his rifle he approached nearer to his foe, who made defense with his TOMA-HAWK. Smith shot him In the head the ball passed through a wool hat which he wore, then took a HATCHET and cleft his skull. He took the HAT, the Gun, and this POWDERHORN as Trophies. In cleaving his skull, he cut a gash through the wool hat—it was mended and worn by the sons of William Smith passing from an older to a younger in fact it would not wear out,—the owner determined he would have a NEW HAT, so he secretly made way with it, it was never found, but the parents of the boy punished him by allowing him to go bare-headed during a long period. The gun was changed to a percussion lock and disappeared—the HORN alone remains.

A difficulty now calls for solution, the horn is one belonging to a WHITE man, how did an Indian get possession? ANSWER: The RECORDS of the PALA-TINE committee of SAFETY, which still exist, show that CLEMENTS were Loyalists (Tories) that they were charged with treasonable practices, see Vol. I Pg. 514 Simms Frontiersmen of New York hence one may infer that both the Gun & the Powder horn were loaned to that Indian for use against the Militia. One certainty exists, their use caused the death of General Herkimer & the death of the INDIAN who carried them. The horn is now owned by Mrs. J. A. Smith Dillenback (A descendant of William Smith who captured it) She resided at St. JOHNSVILLE Montgomery County 1890 when the same was sketched.—by RUFUS A. GRIDER of Canajoharie, N.Y.

At the bottom of the sketch of the horn is written a separate line, "was a Private in Colonel Peter Bellinger's Regiment, Captain Staring's Company, N.Y.

State levies." Captain Heinrich Staring was my fourth great-grandfather.

Some of the above tradition was corrected in a *St. Johnsville Enterprise and News* article dated January 29, 1941. The newspaper article states that Henry Smith Sr., not William, deserves credit for shooting the Indian who wounded General Herkimer. William Smith, although a soldier in the Revolution, would have been only seventeen years old at the time of the Oriskany Battle, seemingly too young to serve as the general's aide.

The same article, by citing an 1884 account of the incident, also provides slightly different particulars—drawn from family tradition—in describing the shooting incident and a description of the horn.

> The horn is large in size, well preserved and highly engraved With carvings of different patterns, birds, trees, fishes, antelopes, deer, cows, etc., together with this inscription, 'Ames Clement 1757' the first being the Indian's name and the latter probably the year it was made ready for use.

The gentleman who wrote the above account omitted the "I" at the beginning of the name on the horn. In the eighteenth century the letter "J" when used as the first letter of a proper name, was often written as "I". This is clearly visible on the horn, hence the first name should be "James."

We owe Rufus Grider a debt of gratitude for his pioneer efforts in the appreciation of engraved American powder horns. He sketched hundreds of eighteenth and nineteenth century powder horns in his own unique style—which was to "unroll" the horn so that the decoration on the entire surface was visible—and often included a brief biography of the original owner and other pertinent information concerning the history of the horn.

A self-taught artist, Grider moved from Lititz, Pennsylvania to Canajoharie, New York in 1883, where he not only taught art in the public schools but also painted in watercolors a series of engraved powder horns and other historical subjects. These paintings are nearly always called "Grider drawings"; many are now owned by the New York Historical Society, New York, New York. Rufus Grider left us an invaluable record of historic information and his name should become familiar again to those interested in New York Colonial and Revolutionary War history.

To answer his own question, Grider surmised that Clement had lent his gun and powder horn to an Indian to use during the Oriskany Battle. However, there may be another explanation which should now be investigated; the "Indian" was really a white man dressed and painted in Indian fashion.

It has been shown that at least a part of the Clement family were Tories (Loyalists - British supporters). In "The Burning of the Valleys" by Gavin Watt, Lieutenant Joseph Clement is shown to have served with the British Six Nations Indian Department in 1780. Indian Department rangers were at Oriskany in 1777. After the battle, Lt. Colonel John Butler wrote to Sir Guy Carleton (Governor of Quebec), August 15, 1777, "myself with the Indians and 20 rangers were posted to flank them (General Herkimer's militia) in the woods." The commander of the Indians for the St. Leger expedition, Daniel Claus, wrote to British

Secretary of War Knox on October 16, 1777, of the Indians who had their camp plundered by Colonel Willett's sortie," and took away the Indians packs, with their clothes, wampum and silver work, they having gone in their shirts, or naked to action..." Later in the report Claus states, "The origin of Rangers since the late Sir William Johnson's time was to intermix them with the Indians when on service..."

Author Dick LaCrosse's notes on frontier clothing describe the dress of the Eastern Woodland Indians; "Their dress consists of skins... or a blanket, a shirt of linen... breechcloth, leggings, reaching half way up the thigh, and fastened to a belt, with moccasins on their feet. They use no ligatures that might obstruct the circulation of their blood, or agility of their limbs. They shave their head.... When they prepare for an engagement they paint themselves black, and fight naked."

We can now reliably say that the Indian Department rangers fought with the Indians in battle, and we have a good idea that typical Indian battle dress of the period was scant at best.

Referring to LaCrosse's biography of Schoharie rifleman John Wilbur, we also have evidence that whites dressed as Indians in battle. Wilbur was a member of a small body of rangers, commanded by David Elerson, in service at the Schoharie middle fort, October 1780. Wilbur confronted a man dressed in Indian fashion who was catching a horse. When asked what party he belonged to, the man answered "the Indian party" and was instantly shot by the rifleman. Both the dead man and another also shot that October day purported to be Indians, but were proven to be "blue-eyed Indians"—Tories from the Albany area dressed as Indians.

Now we can conclude with certainty that Tories sometimes dressed in Indian garb (as did some American rangers and riflemen) when they went out to perform their duties in the war. Perhaps the "Indian" who was killed by Mr. Smith at the Oriskany Battle was actually one of these disguised whites. For the life of me, I cannot imagine a native of the American forest wearing a wool hat—in battle—in the heat of August.

This is a wonderfully intriguing story; you know now what I know, which is a great deal more than only three months ago. Personally, I feel that either James Clement or a close family relative, perhaps a son, shot and wounded General Herkimer during the Oriskany Battle. Only future research, new information—and perhaps a little luck—will reveal the truth.

—Alan E. Sterling
August 1998

Appendix II

Tryon County Militiaman, illustration by David Yahnke

The Organization of the Tryon County Militia, 1775-1777

The Militia and the Minutemen

The Tryon County Militia has for some time been misrepresented as a bunch of half-trained farmers who only met for military training once or twice a year. This generalization greatly misrepresents the amount of training and drilling these units received in the early part of the war.

The militia that were with General Herkimer's brigade can be grouped into three categories: common militia, Minutemen, and rangers. The common militia and the Minutemen were raised along similar lines; as such I will discuss these two groups first. The ranger companies were full-time militia forces usually raised for six to twelve months and will be discussed as a subchapter.

On August 22, 1775, the Provincial Congress of the State of New York adopted the militia bill set forth by the Second Continental Congress on May 10 of 1775. This ordinance required that: ". . . Every County, City, Manor, Town, Precinct, and District within this Colony (where the same is not already done) be divided into districts or seats by their respective Committees in such manner, that out of each may be formed a military Company, ordinarily to consist of about 83 able-bodied men, Officers included, between 16 and 60 years of age."

The officers of the company were to consist of one captain, two lieutenants, one ensign, four sergeants, four corporals, one clerk, one drummer, and one fifer. The officers were to be elected by ballot and the elections were to be supervised by two members of the Committee of Safety. This law also required one-fourth of the militia to be Minutemen, and if they could not fill the ranks with volunteers, they were authorized to draft men from the militia to fill out those ranks. The Minutemen were organized into their own companies, were formed into their own battalions, and elected their own officers. All of New York's militia companies were organized into regiments which were to consist of not less than five and no more than ten companies.[1]

Tryon County was originally brigaded with Albany County and made up the Second Brigade of New York State Militia. On September 5, 1776, the Provincial Congress of New York authorized Tryon County's Militia to be its own brigade. The Provincial Congress appointed Nicholas Herkimer brigadier general of the Tryon County Brigade.[2] Considering Brigadier General Herkimer's commission came from this period, it appears he was for a time the junior brigadier general of the New York State Militia.

Each man was required to equip himself with the following articles for militia duty: One good musket or firelock; a bayonet, sword, or tomahawk; a steel ramrod; a worm; priming wire and brush fitted thereto; a cartouch box to contain 23 rounds of cartridges; 12 flints; and knapsack.

Any man who did not have the requisite equipment was subject to the following fines: Deficient musket or firelock – 5 shillings; deficient a sword, tomahawk, or bayonet – 1 shilling; deficient a cartridge box, cartridge or bullet pouch – sixpence.

Fines were to be adjudged by the captain with appeal to the Committee of

Safety. The collected fines were to be used by the captain to purchase both fifes and drums for their companies. Every able bodied man between 16 and 50 years of age were to be so armed. Those over 50 years of age were encouraged to also be armed in the same manner.

The militia was required to drill on the first Monday of each month for four hours. This drill was to be conducted at the captain's house as this was, by law, considered their "parade."

The Minutemen were organized upon a somewhat different footing. The Minutemen's companies were divided into four subdivisions for drill purposes. The subdivisions were to meet once a week. Each subdivision was to muster under one (presumably the physically closest) of the company officers and to drill for four hours. Battalions of Minutemen were to be composed of seven companies. The Minutemen were also to drill on Mondays, however, after December 21, 1775, their drill schedule was reduced to two drills a month for which they were to be paid the same wages as Continental Soldiers for their service.

Both the militia and the Minutemen were required to muster as a regiment or battalion at least two days every year. Also the field officers (i.e. majors, lieutenant colonels, and colonels) of the battalions or regiments were required to choose a place of assembly for their regiments at a convenient place. Colonel Bellinger set the 4th Battalion of Tryon County Militia's place of assembly "by the church at Kingsland's at the south side of the River." This appears to be the Fort Herkimer Church. Written commissions for the officers of the 4th Tryon County Battalion were not issued until after March 21, 1776.

Failure to attend a militia muster was considered a serious matter. The following fines were assessed for missing muster: colonel, 5 pounds; lieutenant colonel, 4 pounds; major, 3 pounds; captains, lieutenant, adjutants, 30 shillings; ensigns, quartermasters, 20 shillings; sergeants, corporals, drummers, fifers, privates, 10 shillings.

These fines doubled with every missed muster. Even worse, those who missed three musters were held up as an "enemy of his Country." These punishments were executed as illustrated in the minutes and correspondence of the Tryon County Committee of Safety. The fines collected for missing musters were to be used toward the purchase of arms and accouterments for those people who could not afford them. Those who refused to serve or were among the "disaffected" people and slaves were required to serve march with the militia.

The Ranger Companies of Tryon County

The ranger companies were first raised by order of the Provincial Congress of the State of New York on July 23, 1776. The counties of Albany, Tryon, Ulster, Charlotte, Gloucester, and Cumberland were ordered to raise companies of rangers. Tryon County was to raise three companies for a total ranging force of two hundred and one men. The rangers were to be arranged in companies consisting of one captain, two lieutenants, three sergeants, three corporals, and fifty-eight privates.

The rangers were paid the same as Continental troops. They were to receive a bounty of $25 for each private and non-commissioned officer. The rangers were to purchase their rations for which they were given: captain – 16 shillings per week; lieutenant – 14 shillings per week; non-commissioned officers and privates – 10 shillings per week.

The authorization of this force required that all rangers (officers and enlisted men included) supply themselves with the following articles: musket or firelock, powder horn, bullet pouch, tomahawk, blanket, and knapsack.

The rangers were raised for service in their home counties "unless called forth for the defence of a neighboring County or State by the Mutual Consent of the bordering County Committees of the respective Counties or States." Officers for the ranger companies were appointed with the recommendation of the county committees. To facilitate the raising of the rangers, the Provincial Congress on July 24, 1776, gave one-half the bounty money for the rangers to be raised to the deputies of the county at the Congress. Tryon County received 960 pounds sterling.

Tryon County appointed as captains Marcus Demotte (Mark Demuth), Christian Kitman (Christian Gettman), and John Winn. This ranger establishment was dissolved on March 27, 1777.

On July 17, 1777, the Provincial Congress of the State of New York authorized the raising of two companies of rangers in each of the following counties: Tryon, Albany, and Ulster. These companies were to consist of one captain, one lieutenant, four sergeants, four corporals, one drum or fife, and ninety privates. These rangers were instructed to find their own arms and accouterments and were to be allowed the same pay as Continental soldiers. The rangers were allowed the following pay for rations: captains – 16 shillings per week; lieutentants – 14 shillings per week; non-commissioned officers and privates – 10 shillings per week. Unless "when it shall be thought more expedient by the Officer commanding the said Companies to have the same supplied with rations, in which case no subsidence money shall be allowed, but the same shall be applied by the Commanding Officer to the purchase of such rations."

The second establishment of rangers was raised by Captains John Harper and James Clyde, assisted by Lieutenants Alexander Harper and John Campbell, respectively. Captain (also Colonel) Harper was encouraged to "recruit as fast as possible" and to properly station them. History records that three of the rangers were dispatched on the night of August 5, 1777. They were Captain Mark Damuth of Deerfield, Han Yost Folts, and Adam Helmer. Needless to say, we are sure some of the rangers were with Herkimer's brigade.

The rangers were under orders to "be cautious of making any attack upon the Savages or pursue any measures that bring on an Indian war, unless absolutely Necessary."[3]

—Joseph S. Robertaccio

1   "Documents Relating to the Colonial History of the State of New York." Vol. XV. 1887: ed. Berthold Fernow. Weed, Parsons and Company, Printers. pp. 30-34.
2   "Proceedings of the New York Historical Society" for the year 1845. p. 172.

Appendix III

Photo by James Morrison

Enactment of Tryon County Militia on the march

MUSTER ROLL OF THE BATTLE OF ORISKANY
AUGUST 6, 1777

The following information was compiled from the research of James Morrison of Gloversville, New York, and organized by Joseph Robertaccio of Utica, New York.

The rank and hometown of each individual is given, as well as their battle status noted by the following key: DOW, died of wounds; K, killed; C, captured; W, wounded.

COMMAND STAFF

Herkimer, Nicholas	Brigadier General, Danube, DOW Aug. 17, 1777
Frey, John	Brigade Major, Palatine Bridge, W, C
Younglove, Moses	Brigade Surgeon, Minden, W, C

1ST BATTALION, CANAJOHARIE DISTRICT

Cox, Ebenezer, Sr.	Colonel, Minden, K
Seeber, William	Lt. Colonel, Minden, W, DOW Sept. 1, 1777
Campbell, Samuel	1st Major, Cherry Valley
Clyde, Samuel	2nd Major, Cherry Valley
Pickard, John	Quartermaster (Regiment), Canajoharie, W
Bowman, Peter	Captain, K
Copeman, Abraham	Captain, Minden
Crouse, Robert	Captain, Minden, K
Dieffendorf, Henery	Captain, Minden, K
Seeber, Jacob W.	Captain, Canajoharie, W, DOW at Ft. Herkimer
Van Evera, Rynier	Captain, Canajoharie
Weser, Nicholas	Captain
Whitaker, Thomas	Captain
Bradt, Henry	1st Lieutenant, W
Campbell, Robert	1st Lieutenant, Cherry Valley, K
Dieffendorf, Jacob	1st Lieutenant, Minden
Resner, George	1st Lieutenant, Minden, K
Sommer, Peter	1st Lieutenant, Sharon
Van Alstyne, Martin	1st Lieutenant, Canajoharie
Dygert, Jost	2nd Lieutenant, Fall Hill
Grinnall, James	2nd Lieutenant, K
Gros, Lawrence	2nd Lieutenant, Minden
Heath, Nataniel	2nd Lieutenant, K
House, Jost	2nd Lieutenant, Minden
Klock, Adam	2nd Lieutenant, K
Seeber, John	2nd Lieutenant, Minden
Seeber, Severius	2nd Lieutenant, Canajoharie, K
Seeber, William	2nd Lieutenant, Canajoharie
Arndt, Abraham	Ensign, Minden
Horning, Sr., Dederick	Ensign, C
Pickerd, John	Ensign, Springfield
Seeber, Adolph	Ensign, Minden, K
Bardt, Christian	Sergeant, K
Dunlop, John	Sergeant, Cherry Valley
Garlock, Charles	Sergeant, K

Petry, Marcus	Sergeant, K
Petry, Nicholas	Sergeant, K
Ehle, Peter	Corporal, Canajoharie
Elwood, Isaac	Corporal, W
Marinus, William	Corporal, K
Pickerd, Adolph	Corporal, Springfield, W
Young, Godfrey	Corporal, Canajoharie, W
Bardt, Nicholas	Private
Becker, Henry	Private
Bellinger, William	Private
Bush, George	Private, Springfield
Casler, John	Private, Canajoharie
Countryman, Conrad	Private
Countryman, Fredrick	Private
Countryman, John	Private
Cox, William	Private
Crouse, George	Private, Minden
Davis, Thomas	Private, Springfield, K
Dickson, James	Private, Cherry Valley
Dickson, William	Private, Cherry Valley
Dieffendorf, John	Private, Minden
Dunckle, Garret	Private, Freysbush
Dunckle, George	Private, Freysbush
Dunckle, John	Private, Freysbush
Dunckle, Nicholas	Private, Freysbush
Dunckle, Peter	Private, Freysbush (all Dunckles were brothers)
Dunlop, William	Private, Cherry Valley
Dusler, _____	Private, Danube, K
Dusler, John	Private, Danube
Ehle, Peter	Private, C
Ehle, William	Private, Canajoharie
Failing, Henry	Private, Canajoharie, W
Failing, Henry Nicholas	Private
Failing, Jacob	Private, Canajoharie
Flint, Adam	Private
Flint, Alexander	Private, Canajoharie
Flint, Cornelius	Private, Canajoharie
Flint, John	Private, Canajoharie
Flint, Robert	Private, Bowman's Cre
Flock, John	Private
Garlock, Adam	Private, Canajoharie
Geortner, George	Private, Canajoharie
Hawn, Conrad	Private, K
Helmer, John G.	Private, Canajoharie
Hoover, Jacob	Private
Horning, Adam	Private
Horning, George	Private
Horning, John	Private
Horning, Lambert	Private
Horning, Dedrick, Jr.	Private
House, Conrad	Private, K
House, Henry	Private, K
Jackson, Joseph	Private, K
Johnson, Witter	Private

Jordan, Adam	Private
Keller, Jacob	Private, Minden
Keller, Solomon	Private, K
Levy, Michael	Private, Canajoharie, K
Lintner, George	Private, Minden
Longshore, Solomon	Private, Canajoharie
Markell, William	Private, K
Matthias, Hendrick	Private, K
Miller, John	Private, Minden
Moyer, John Jacob	Private, Minden
Ohr, Jacob	Private, Minden
Pickerd, Nicholas	Private, Canajoharie
Price, Adam	Private, Canajoharie, K
Rathenhower, Godfrey	Private, K
Ribson, Matthias	Private, K
Roth, John	Private, Minden
Sanders, Henry	Private, Minden, W
Seeber, Henry	Private, Canajoharie, W
Seeber, James	Private, K
Shaffer, William	Private, W
Sits, John	Private
Snyder, John	Private, Minden
Sparks, Pearl	Private, W
Van Alstyne, Martin G.	Private, Canajoharie
Van Alstyne, Phillip	Private, Canajoharie
Van Deusen, George	Private, Canajoharie
Van Evera, John	Private, Canajoharie
Vatterly, Henry	Private, K
Waggoner, George	Private, Canajoharie, W
Waggoner, Jacob	Private, Canajoharie
Walrath, Jacob	Private, Canajoharie
Westerman, Peter	Private, Minden, K
Wolleber, John	Private
Wright, Jacob	Private, Canajoharie, W
Yordan, John P.	Private, Canajoharie (brother of Adam Jordan)
Young, Joseph	Private
Zoller, Andrew	Private, Minden, C
Zoller, Jacob	Private, K

2ND BATTALION, PALATINE DISTRICT

Klock, Jacob	Colonel, St. Johnsville
Waggoner, Peter Sr.	Lt. Colonel, Town of Palatine
Van Slyke, Hermanus	1st Major, K
Paris, Isaac, Sr.	2nd Major, Stone Arabia, K
VanVeghten, Anthony	Adjutant
Breadbake, John	Captain, Palatine, W
Dillenback, Andrew	Captain, Palatine, K
Dygert, John	Captain, Stone Arabia, K
Fox, Christopher P.	Captain, Palatine, K
Fox, Christopher Wm.	Captain, Palatine, W
Helmer, Philip	Captain, Manheim
Hess, John	Captain, Palatine
House, Christian	Captain, St. Johnsville
Keyser, John	Captain, Manheim

Richter, Nicholas	Captain, Tillsborough (Ephratah)
Bellinger, Adam	1st Lieutenant
Loucks, Peter	1st Lieutenant, Palatine
Zeely, John	1st Lieutenant, Stone Arabia
Bellinger, John, Jr.	2nd Lieutenant, Palatine
Ecker, Jacob	2nd Lieutenant, Stone Arabia
Miller, Henry	2nd Lieutenant, Palatine
Smith, George	2nd Lieutenant, Palatine
Waggoner, Peter, Jr.	2nd Lieutenant, Palatine
Coppernoll, Richard	Ensign, Palatine
Gray, Samuel	Ensign, Stone Arabia
Scholl, John	Ensign, Tillsborough, Ephratah
Timmerman, Henry	Ensign, St. Johnsville, W
Comb, Urial	Sergeant, K
Cook, John	Sergeant, Palatine, W
Ritter, Johannes	Sergeant, Manheim, K
Snell, George	Sergeant, Stone Arabia, K
Snell, Peter	Sergeant, Palatine
Suits, Peter	Sergeant, Palatine
Fink, Christian	Corporal, Palatine, K
Kring, Lodowick	Corporal, Tillsborough (Ephratah)
Timmerman, John	Corporal, Palatine
Walrath, Jacob H.	Corporal, Palatine, W
Snell, Jacob	Fifer, Stone Arabia
Snell, Jacob, Jr.	Fifer, K
Van Slyke, Nicholas	Fifer, Palatine, K
Bauder, Melchert	Private, Palatine
Baun, John George	Private, K
Beeler, Jacob	Private
Beeler, Joseph	Private
Bellinger, Fredrick	Private, K
Bellinger, John Frederick	Private, K
Bellington, James	Private, K
Bellington, Samuel	Private, Palatine, K
Bishop, Charles	Private, W
Boyer, John P.	Private
Casselman, John	Private
Cook, Severinus	Private
Cramer, Jacob	Private
Deharsh, Philip	Private
Dorn, Peter	Private
Dygert, George	Private
Dygert, Peter	Private
Eacker, Nicholas	Private, Stone Arabia
Egenbrode, John	Private (Eigenbrote, Eigenbroat)
Eigenbroat, Peter	Private
Empie, Jacob	Private, Palatine, K
Failing, Jacob J.	Private, St. Johnsville
Fink, Christian	Private, Palatine
Fink, William	Private, Palatine
Flanders, Dennis Augustus	Private, Palatine
Fos, Peter	Private
Fox, Christopher W.	Private, Palatine
Fox, Peter W.	Private, Palatine

Fox, William W.	Private
Frealing, Jacob	Private
Freligh, Valatine	Private, Palatine
Fry, Jacob	Private
Gago, George	Private, St. Johnsville, K
Garlock, Peter	Private
Garrison, John	Private
Garter, John, Jr.	Private
Getman, Thomas	Private, Palatine
Gram, John	Private
Gramps, John P.	Private
Gray, Nicholas	Private, K
Hart, Daniel	Private, Palatine
Henner, Peter	Private, K (Helmer)
Hoover, John	Private, Manheim
Huffnagel, Christian	Private, K
Keller, Andrew	Private, Palatine
Keyser, Bernard	Private, Manheim
Keyser, Han Yost	Private, Manheim
Keyser, Henry	Private, Manheim
Keyser, Michael	Private, Manheim
Kilts, Conrad	Private, Stone Arabia
Klock, Jacob	Private, Palatine
Klock, John	Private, St. Johnsville
Lampman, Henry	Private, K
Lampman, Peter	Private, Palatine, W
Leathers, Christian	Private, Palatine
Leathers, John	Private, Palatine
Lentz, Jacob	Private
Lentz, John	Private
Lepper, Jacob	Private, K
Lepper, Wyant	Private, Stone Arabia
Lonas, John	Private
Loucks, Adam	Private, Stone Arabia
Loucks, Adam A.	Private
Loucks, Henry	Private, Palatine
Loucks, Joseph	Private
Loucks, Peter	Private, C
Loucks, William	Private, Stone Arabia, W
Markell, Jacob	Private
Martin, Alexander	Private, W
Merckly, William	Private, Palatine, K
Miller, John	Private
Moyer, John	Private
Nellis, Christain	Private, Palatine
Nellis, John D.	Private, Palatine
Nellis, Phillip	Private, Palatine, W
Nelson, Paul	Private, Palatine
Nestle, Paul	Private, Manheim
Newman, Joseph	Private, Manheim
Paris, Peter	Private, Palatine, K (son of Maj. Isaac Paris)
Philips, James	Private, W
Pickerd, Bartholomew	Private
Putman, Martinus	Private, K

Rasbell, Frederick	Private, Palatine, W
Rickard, Jacob	Private
Saltsman, John	Private, W
Shite, Peter	Private, Tillsborough (Ephratah)
Shults, George	Private, Stone Arabia
Shults, Henry	Private, Palatine
Shults, Jacob	Private
Shults, John	Private
Smith, George	Private, Palatine
Smith, Nicholas, Sr.	K
Snell, Frederick	Snellsbush, K
Snell, Jacob	Snellsbush, K
Snell, Jacob F.	Snellsbush, K
Snell, John, Sr.	Stone Arabia, K
Snell, Joseph	K
Snell, Suffernus	Snellsbush, K
Spank, Nebel	W
Sponable, John	C
Spraker, John	Stone Arabia
Strader, Nicholas	Palatine
Suits, Peter J.	Private, Palatine
Sulback, Garret	W
Suts, John I.	
Thum, Adam	St. Johnsville
Timmerman, Henry	Palatine
Van Slyke, Jacobus	Manheim
Visger, John	Manheim
Waffle, John Henry	Palatine
Walrath, Garret	C
Walrath, Henry J.	C
Walrath, Nicholas	W
Walrath, Peter	Palatine
Walter, George	W
Windecker, Frederick	Manheim
Windecker, Nicholas	Manheim
Woelber, Nicholas	C
Wormuth, John	Palatine
Young, Jacob A.	Palatine
Zimmerman, Conrad	

3RD BATTALION, MOHAWK DISTRICT

Visscher, Frederick	Colonel, Dadanascara, W
Veeder, Volkert	Lt. Colonel, Fonda
Bliven, John	1st Major, Florida, W, C
Newkirk, John	2nd Major, Florida
Van Horne, Abraham	Quartermaster (Regiment)
Conyne, Peter	Adjutant, Tribes Hill
Davis, John James	Captain, Town of Moha, K
DeGraff, Emanuel	Captain, Amsterdam
Fonda, Jellis	Captain, Town of Moha
Gardinier, Jacob	Captain, Glen, W
Mabee, Hermanus	Captain
McMaster, David	Captain, Florida
Pettingell, Samuel	Captain, Florida, K

Visscher, John	Captain, Dadanascara
Yates, Robert Abraham	Captain, Root
Hanson, Henry	1st Lieutenant, Town of Moha
Printop, Joseph	1st Lieutenant, Glen
Pruyne, Francis	1st Lieutenant
Quackenboss, Abraham	1st Lieutenant, Glen
Snook, William	1st Lieutenant, Florida
Swart, Josiah J.	1st Lieutenant
Veeder, Abraham	1st Lieutenant, Florida
Wemple, John	1st Lieutenant, Tribes Hill
Hall, William	2nd Lieutenant, Glen
Marlat, John	2nd Lieutenant, Mohawk
Newkirk, Garret	2nd Lieutenant, Florida
Putman, Victor C.	2nd Lieutenant
Lewis, Hendrick	Ensign, Currytown, W
Putman, Francis	Ensign, Charleston
Van Bracklen, Garret S.	Ensign
Van Eps, Charles	Ensign
Van Horne, Thomas	Ensign, Florida
VanVeghten, Dedrick	Ensign, Florida
Covenhoven, Peter	Sergeant, Glen, W
Van Eps, Evert	Sergeant, Glen, W
Tuthill, Stephen	Corporal, Florida, K
Clement, Lambert	Private, Mohawk
Collier, Jacob	Private, Florida
Cone, Samuel	Private
Connelly, Hugh	Private, Florida
Covenhoven, Cornelius	Private, Glen
Covenhoven, Isaac	Private, Glen
Covenhoven, John	Private, Glen
Cromwell, Hermanus	Private, Fonda
Davis, Benjamin	Private, Mohawk, K
Davis, Martinus	Private, Mohawk, K
Dockstader, George	Private, Mohawk
Dockstader, John	Private, Mohawk
Dockstader, John N.	Private, Johnstown
Dockstader, Leonard	Private, Mohawk
Everson, Adam	Private
Everson, John	Private
Fonda, John	Private
Frank, Adam	Private, Glen
Frank, John	Private, K
Frank, Andrew, Jr.	Private, Mohawk, W (all Franks were brothers)
Frederick, Francis	Private, Florida
Gardinier, Nicholas A.	Private, Glen
Gardinier, Samuel	Private, Glen, W
Gray, Silas	Private, Florida
Groot, Petrus	Private, Amsterdam, W, C (held captive until 1807)
Hunt, Timothy	Private, Florida
Lenardson, John	Private, Root
Lewis, John	Private
Martin, Philip	Private, W
Mason, John	Private, Johnstown
McMaster, Hugh	Private, Florida, W

Miller, Adam	Private, Mohawk, W
Mour, George	Private, Glen, W
Mower, Conrad	Private, Currytown
Murray, David	Private, Florida
Newkirk, Jacob	Private, Florida
Pettingell, John	Private, Florida, K
Pettingell, William	Private, Florida
Phillips, Abraham	Private, Fonda
Phillips, Cornelius	Private, Florida, K
Phillips, James	Private, K
Phillips, John	Private, Mohawk
Prime, Peter	Private, K
Pruyne, Lewis	Private, Florida
Putman, Peter	Private, Florida, K
Putman, Richard	Private, Johnstown
Putman, Victor	Private, Tribes Hill
Quackenboss, Nicholas	Private, Glen
Quackenboss, Peter I.	Private, Glen
Sammons, Sampson	Private, Mohawk
Schuyler, William	Private, Florida
Servis, Christian	Private, Florida
Servis, George	Private, Florida
Servis, John	Private, Florida
Spore, John	Private, Florida
Staley, Henry	Private, Florida
Starin, Nicholas	Private, Glen
Staring, Adam	Private, Charleston
Staring, John	Private, Glen
Sternberg, Joseph	Private, Charleston
Stine, George	Private, Florida
Stouets, Philip	Private, Root, K
Terwilliger, James	Private, Florida
Thompson, Henry	Private, Glen
Thornton, James	Private, Florida
Van Antwerp, John, Jr.	Private, Glen, W
Van Eps, John	Private
Van Horne, Cornelius	Private, Florida
Van Horne, Henry	Private, Florida
Van Slyke, Martin	Private, Charleston
Van Slyke, Nicholas	Private, Glen
Veeder, Hendrick	Private
Veeder, John	Private
Visscher, Hermanus	Private, Dadanascara (brother of John & Frederick Visscher)
Vrooman, Hendrick	Private, Mohawk
Young, Peter	Private, Florida

4TH BATTALION, KINGSLAND & GERMAN FLATTS DISTRICT

Bellinger, Peter	Colonel, Little Falls
Bellinger, Frederick	Lt. Colonel, German Flatts, C
Eisenlord, John	1st Major, Schuyler, K
Clapsaddle, Augustus	2nd Major, K
Steel, Rudolph	Quartermaster (Regiment), German Flatts
Petry, William	Surgeon, Fort Herkimer, W
Dygert, William	Captain, German Flatts

Eckler, Henry	Captain, Kille (Chyle)
Herter, Henry	Captain, German Flatts
Huber, Henry	Captain, Little Falls, C
Ittig, Michael	Captain, C
Staring, Henry	Captain, Schuyler
Shoemaker, Rudolph	Captain
Small, Jacob	Captain, Fall Hill
Baschauer, Jacob	1st Lieutenant
Petry, Richard Marcus	1st Lieutenant, Little Falls, K
Vols, Jacob	1st Lieutenant, Frankfort
Frank, Frederick	2nd Lieutenant
Helmer, George F.	2nd Lieutenant, Herkimer, W
Petrie, Han Yost	2nd Lieutenant, Herkimer, K
Raspach, Marx	2nd Lieutenant, Kingsland
Campbell, Patrick	Ensign
Hiller, Jacob	Ensign, Fairfield, K
Myers, John	Ensign
Weaver, Peter J.	Ensign, German Flatts
Campbell, John	Sergeant
Cunningham, Andrew	Sergeant, K
Davy, John	Sergeant, K
Frank, John	Sergeant, Kingsland
Petry, Han Yost	Sergeant, W, DOW Aug. 30, 1777
Piper, Andrew	Sergeant, German Flatts
Staring, Adam	Sergeant
Steinway, Arnold	Sergeant, German Flatts, K
Casler, Conrad	Corporal
Iser, Frederick	Corporal, K
Stephens, Frederick	Corporal, K
Wolleber, John	Drummer
Ayer, Frederick	Private, Schulyer, K
Bell, George Henry	Private, Fall Hill, W
Bell, Jacob	Private, K
Bell, Joseph	Private, Fall Hill, K
Bell, Nicholas	Private, Fall Hill, K
Bellinger, Frederick	Private, German Flatts
Bellinger, John	Private, German Flatts
Bellinger, John Frederick	Private, K
Bellinger, Peter	Private
Bellinger, William	Private, German Flatts
Biddleman, Adam	Private
Bowman, Frederick	Private
Bronner, Frederick	Private, Stark
Carl, George	Private
Casler, Adam	Private
Casler, Adolph	Private
Casler, Jacob, Jr.	Private
Casler, Jacob, Sr.	Private
Casler, John, Jr.	Private
Christman, Frederick	Private, Herkimer, W
Clapsaddle, Jacob	Private, German Flatts
Clements, Jacob	Private, Schuyler
Dockstader, John	Private, Herkimer
Dockstader, Peter	Private, German Flatts

Eckler, Christopher	Private, Kyle
Eckler, Leonard	Private, Kyle
Eckler, Peter	Private, Kyle
Eysamen, Stephen	Private
Finster, John	Private, German Flatts
Fox, Frederick	Private
Fox, John	Private
Fox, Philip	Private
Frank, Henry	Private, Frankfort
Geortner, Peter	Private
Getman, Peter	Private, Frankfort
Hadcock, Daniel	Private, Little Falls
Hartman, John Adam	Private, Herkimer
Helmer, Frederick	Private, German Flatts, K
Herkimer, George	Private, Danube
Herkimer, Henry	Private, German Flatts
Herkimer, Joseph	Private
Herter, John	Private, German Flatts
Hess, Augustus, Sr.	Private, German Flatts
Hess, Conrad	Private, German Flatts
Hess, Frederick	Private
Hess, George	Private
Hess, John	Private, German Flatts, K
Hess, John	Private, W
Hoyer, George Frederick	Private
Hunt, Peter	Private, K
Ittig, Jacob	Private, German Flatts
Ittig, John, Sr.	Private, German Flatts
Lapius, Jacob Abraham	Private
Lighthall, George	Private
Lighthall, Nicholas	Private, German Flatts
Miller, Hendrick	Private
Miller, John	Private
Moyer, Jacob	Private, German Flatts, K
Moyer, Joseph	Private, Herkimer
Orendorff, Frederick	Private
Petry, John	Private, Herkimer, W
Petry, John Mark	Private, German Flatts
Petry, Joseph	Private, Herkimer, K
Phyfer, Andrew	Private, W
Raspach, Frederick	Private, Herkimer, W
Schell, Christian	Private, Schellsbush
Schell, John	Private, Schuyler, W
Schuyler, Philip	Private, K
Sharrar, Christian	Private, Herkimer, K
Shault, Henry	Private, Stark
Shoemaker, John	Private
Shoemaker, Thomas	Private, Herkimer
Smith, Frederick	Private
Smith, George	Private
Staring, Henry	Private, W
Staring, Peter	Private
Vols, Conrad	Private, W
Vols, Peter	Private, Frankfort, K

Weaver, George	Private, German Flatts
Weaver, George Michael	Private
Weaver, Jacob	Private, German Flatts
Widrig, Michael	Private, Schuyler
Wolleber, Abraham	Private, Fort Herkimer
Wolleber, Dederick	Private, Fort Herkimer, K
Wolleber, Johannes	Private, Fort Herkimer, K
Wolleber, Peter	Private, Fort Herkimer
Wrenkle, Lawrance	Private, German Flatts, K

WARRIORS OF THE ONEIDA INDIAN NATION

Lt. Colonel Louis Atayataghronghta
Captain Hanyere Tewahangarahken, W
Polly (Cobus) Tewahangarahken
Lt. Hanyost Tewahangarahken (brother of Cpt. Hanyere)
Captain James Wakarantharaus, W
Blatcop
Henry Cornelius
Thomas Spencer, Cherry Valley, K

ENDNOTES

Chapter One – Centennial
1 Oneida Historical Society, p. 3.
2 *Utica Morning Herald*, Aug. 6, 1877.
3 Oneida Historical Society, p. 15.
4 Ibid., pp. 18-19.
5 Ibid., p. 23.

Chapter Two – The Iroquois
1 Parker, p. 14.
2 Ibid., p. 19.
3 Ibid., p. 20.
4 Ibid., p. 21.
5 Ibid., p. 23.
6 Ibid., p. 30.
7 Bonvillain, p. 33.
8 Ibid., p. 13.
9 Greene, p. 188.
10 Bonvillain, p. 40.
11 Ibid., p. 45.
12 Langer, p. 7.

Chapter Three – The Loyalists
1 Flexner, p. 347.
2 Ibid., p. 233.
3 Ibid., p. 229.
4 Ibid., p. 37.
5 Ibid., p. 53.
6 Langer, p. 6.
7 Flexner, p. 62.
8 Ibid., p. 70.
9 Tilberg, p. 4.
10 Gifford, p. 15.
11 Ibid., p. 16.
12 Flexner, p. 292.

Chapter Four – The Patriots
1 Palatine Society, p. 5.
2 Ibid., p. 1.
3 Ibid., p. 6.
4 Ibid., p. 23.
5 Ibid., p. 27.
6. Ibid., p. 29.
7 Ibid., p. 64.
8 Greene., p. 671.

Chapter Five – Revolution
1 Meltzer, p. 37.
2 Ibid., p. 38.
3 Ibid., p. 39.
4 Ibid., p. 42.
5 McDowell, p. 30.
6 Meltzer, p. 45.
7 Ibid., p. 50.
8 Greene., p. 689.
9 Kelsay, p. 123.
10 Greene, p. 714.
11 Ibid., p. 718.
12 Lancaster, p. 69.
13 McDowell, p. 41.
14 Strobeck, p. 23.
15 Greene, p. 729.
16 Ibid, p. 755.
17 Ibid., pp. 762-763.
18 Graymont, p. 50.
19 Ibid., p. 58.
20. Blum, p. 101.
21. Lancaster, p. 138.

Chapter Six – The March
1 Furneaux, p. 23.
2 Luzader, p. 9.
3 Scott, p. 33.
4 Greene, p. 789.
5 Kelsay, p. 165.
6 Ibid., p. 199.
7 Greene, p. 790.
8. Clinton, pp. 164-165.
9 Greene, p. 794.
10 Thomas, p. 22.
11 Ibid., p. 30.
12 Scott, p. 162.
13 Ibid., pp. 177-178.
14 Lowenthal, p. 37.
15 Clinton, pp. 171-172.
16 Greene, p. 796.
17 Simms, p. 69.

Chapter Seven – The Battle
1 Robertaccio, p. 10.

2   Frederic, p. 372.
3   Robertaccio, p. 17.
4   Simms, p. 102.
5   Greene, p. 839.
6   Ibid., p. 839.
7   Ibid., p. 837.
8   Ibid., p. 836.
9   Robertaccio, p. 17.
10   Greene, p. 798.
11   Draper, pp. 196-197.
12   Simms, pp. 108-109.
13   McDonald, pp. 34-37.
14   Greene, p. 835.
15   Simms, p. 98.
16   Ibid., p. 75.

Chapter Eight – Aftermath
1   Greene, p. 835.
2   Ibid., p. 840.
3   *Utica Daily Herald*, July 30, 1883.
4   Ibid.
5   Scott, p. 195.
6   Ibid., p. 239.

7   Ibid., pp. 240-241.
8   Clinton, pp. 209-210.
9   Scott, p. 248.
10   Ibid., p. 251.
11   Robertaccio, p. 8.
12   Scott, p. 268.
13   Ibid., p. 275.
14   Ibid., p. 253.
15   Ibid., p. 270.
16   Ibid., p. 274.
17   Ibid., p. 289.
18   Ibid., p. 293.
19   Stanley, p. 14.
20   Scott, p. 294.
21   NYS Historical Society, p. 29.
22   Oneida Hist. Society, pp. 123-125.
23   Clinton, p. 671.
24   Stone, p. 295.
25   Robertaccio, p. 24.
26   Ibid., p. 25.
27   Ibid., p. 26.
28   Ibid., p. 27.
29   Stone, pp. 118-119.
30   Robertaccio, p. 28.

Bibliography

Adams, Spencer L. *The Longhouse of the Iroquois.* Skaneateles, NY: Fairview Farm, 1944.

Barker, William. *Early Families of Herkimer County.* Baltimore Genealogical Publishing Co., 1986.

Best, Tharratt. *A Soldier of Oriskany.* Boonville, New York: Willard Press, 1935.

Blum, John. *The National Experience.* New York: Harcourt, Brace & Jovanovich, 1963.

Bonvillain, Nancy. *The Mohawk.* New York: Chelsea House, 1992.

Campbell, William. *Annals of Tryon County.* New York: J. & J. Harper, 1831.

Clarke, T. Wood. *The Bloody Mohawk.* New York: The Macmillan Co., 1940.

Clinton, George. "Public Papers." New York & Albany: State of New York, 1900.

Cobb, Hubbard. *American Battlefields.* New York: Macmillan, 1995.

Colden, Cadwallader. *The History of the Five Nations.* New York: New Amsterdam Book Co., 1902.

Cookinham, Henry. *History of Oneida County.* Chicago: S.J. Clarke Pub. Co., 1912.

Cowan, Phoebe Strong. *The Herkimers and Schuylers.* Albany: Gold Manielli Sons, 1903.

Cronau, Rudolf. *German Achievements in America.* New York: R. Cronau, 1916.

Dawson, Henry. *Battles of the United States by Sea and Land.* New York: Johnson Fry and Co., 1858.

DeWitt, Vera. *American Patriots at the Battle of Oriskany.* Kenmore, NY: DeWitt, 1976. Self-published book.

Draper, Lyman C. Manuscripts and records held by University of Wisconsin Archives.

Durant, Samuel W. *History of Oneida County.* Philadelphia: Everts & Fariss, 1878.

Eckert, Allan. *Wilderness War.* Boston: Little, Brown, 1978.

Elting, John. *The Battles of Saratoga.* Monmouth Beach, NJ: Philip Freneau Press, 1977.

Edmonds, Walter. *Drums Along the Mohawk.* Boston: Little, Brown, 1936.

Flexner, James. *Mohawk Baronet.* New York: Harper, 1959.

Frederick, Harold. *In the Valley.* New York: Charles Scribner's Sons, 1890.

Furneaux, Rupert. *Saratoga.* New York: Stein and Day, 1971.

Gehring, Charles. "Agriculture and the Revolution in the Mohawk Valley." Unpublished article.

Gerlach, Don. *Proud Patriot.* Syracuse: Syracuse University Press, 1987.

Gifford, Stanley. *Fort William Henry.* Gifford, 1955. Self-published book.

Graymont, Barbara. *The Iroquois.* New York: Chelsea House, 1988.

———. *The Iroquois in the American Revolution.* Syracuse: Syracuse University Press, 1992.

Greene, Nelson. *The Mohawk Valley.* Chicago: S.J. Clarke, 1925.

Hagerty, Gilbert. *Massacre at Fort Bull.* Providence: Mowbray Co., 1971.

Hanson, Lee. *Casemates and Cannonballs.* Washington: U.S. Dept. of Interior, National Park Service, 1975.

Hibbert, Christopher. *Redcoats and Rebels.* New York: Norton, 1990.

Hislop, Codman. *The Mohawk.* New York: Rinehart, 1948.

Hubbard, J. Niles. *Red Jacket and His People.* Albany: Joel Mamelli Sons, 1886.

Jacobs. Henry. *The German Emigration to America.* Lancaster, Pa.: The Society, 1898.

Jones, Pomroy. *Annals and Recollections of Oneida County.* Rome, NY: Pomroy, 1851.

Keeler, M. Paul. *One Quarter Mile to Go*. Keeler, 1978. Self-published book.

Kelly, Joe. *USS Oriskany*. Utica, NY: Good Times Publishing, 1997.

Kelsay, Isabel. *Joseph Brant*. Syracuse: Syracuse University Press, 1984.

Langer, Howard. *American Indian Quotations*. Westport, Ct.: Greewood Press, 1996.

Lancaster, Bruce. *From Lexington to Liberty*. Garden City: Doubleday, 1955.

———. *The American Revolution*. New York: American Heritage Publishing Co., 1971.

Lord, Philip. *War Over Walloomscoick*. Albany: State Education Dept., University of the State of New York, 1989.

Lossing, Benson. *The Pictorial Field Book of the Revolution*. New York: Harper & Bros., 1848.

Lowenthal, Larry. *Days of Siege*. New York: Eastern Acorn Press, 1983.

Luzader, John. *Decision on the Hudson*. Washington: Office of Publications, National Park Service, 1975.

May, Robin. *The British Army in North America*. Reading: Osprey Publishing Co., 1974.

McDonald, John. *Great Battlefields of the World*. New York: Collier Books, Macmillan, 1984.

McDowell, Bart. *The Revolutionary War*. Washington: National Geographic Society, 1967.

Meltzer, Milton. *The American Revolutionaries*. New York: Thomas V. Crowell, 1987.

Morrison, James. "A Brief History of the Third Battalion." Unpublished, 1991. Article.

———. "Colonel Jacob Klock's Regiment." Unpublished, 1992. Article.

———. "Life and Times in the Mohawk Valley." Unpublished, 1990. Article.

New York State Historical Society, "Minutes of the Council of Appointments", p. 29.

Nickerson, Hoffman. *The Turning Point of the Revolution*. Boston-New York: Houghton Mifflin, Co., 1928.

Oneida County. *The History of Oneida County*. Oneida County, NY: 1977.

Oneida Historical Society. *Memorial of the Centennial Celebration*. Utica, NY: E.M. Roberts & Co., 1878.

Palatine Society. *The Palatines of New York State*. Palatine Society, Inc., 1953.

Panzeri, Peter. *Little Big Horn 1876*. Reading: Osprey Publishing Co., 1995.

Parker, Arthur. *The Constitution of the Five Nations*. Albany: University of the State of New York, 116.

Patrick, Hazel. *The Mohawk Valley Herkimers*. Herkimer, NY: Herkimer County Historical Society, 1989.

Penrose, Mary. *Compendium of Mohawk Valley Families*. Baltimore Genealogical Publishing, 1988.

Reid, W. Max. *Old Fort Johnson*. New York: Putnam, 1906.

———. *The Mohawk Valley*. New York & London: G.P. Putnam's Sons, 1901.

Robertaccio, Joseph. "A Bloody Morning at Oriskany." Unpublished, 1995. Compendium.

Schramm, Henry. *Central New York*. Norfolk: Downing Co., 1987.

Scott, John Albert. *Fort Stanwix and Oriskany*. Rome, NY: Rome Sentinel Co., 1927.

Simms, Jeptha. *Frontiersmen of New York*. Albany: G.C. Riggs, 1882.

Sleeman, G. Martin. *Early Histories & Descriptions of Oneida County*. Utica, NY: North Country Books, 1990.

Speck, Frank. *The Iroquois*. Bloomfield Hills, MI: Cransbrook Institute of Science, 1945.

Stanley, George. *For Want of a Horse*. 1961.

Stone, William. *Campaign of Lt. Gen. John Burgoyne, etc.* Albany: J. Mansell, 1877.

———. *Orderly Book of Sir John Johnson*. Albany: J. Mansell, 1882.

Strobeck, Katherine. *Mohawk Valley Happenings.* Montgomery County Historical Society, 1990.

———. *The Fort in the Wilderness.* Sylvan Beach, NY: North Country Books, 1978.

Symonds, Craig. *A Battlefield Atlas of the American Revolution.* Baltimore Nautical and Aviation Publishing, 1986.

Thomas, Howard. *Joseph Brant.* Utica, NY: North Country Books, 1984.

Tilberg, Frederick. *Fort Necessity.* 1954.

———. *Marinus Willett.* Prospect, NY: Prospect Books, 1954.

Tommell, Anthony Wayne. *The Brigade Dispatch, Vol. X, No. 2.* The Brigade Dispatch, Newsletter, 1974.

Trevelyan, George. *The American Revolution.* New York: D. McKay Co., 1964.

Utica Morning Herald. August 6 & 7, 1877.

Utley, Robert. *Indian Wars.* New York: American Heritage, 1985.

Wager, Daniel. *Our County and Its People.* New York – Boston: Boston History Co., 1896.

Wallace, Anthony. *The Death and Rebirth of the Seneca..* New York: Knopf, 1969.

Walsh, John. *Vignettes of Old Utica.* Utica, NY: Utica Public Library, 1982.

Wilbur, C. Keith. *The Revolutionary Soldier.* Philadelphia: Chelsea House Publishers, 1969.

Wrong, George. *Washington and His Comrades in Arms.* New Haven: Yale University Press, 1921.

Index of Names

Abercrombie, James, 121, 126
Adams, Deputy Sheriff, 73
Adams, John, 105, 119
Adams, Sam(uel), 95, 99
Allen, Ethan, 104
Amherst, Lord, 78
Ancrum, Maj., 180
Arnold, Benedict, x, 104, 178, 182-184
Arthur, Chester Alan, 9
Axe Carrier, 152, 177

Bacon, William J., 4
Barere, Bertrand, 91
Bedlam, Maj., 127
deBelletre, Gen., 77
Bellinger, Frederick, 131, 146, 179
Bellinger, Peter, 6, 97, 102, 131-132, 146, 152, 155
Bellinger, Peter F., 6
Billington, Samuel, 177
Bird, Lt., 128
Black Feathertail, 152, 177
Black Snake, 148
Blatcop, 146, 160
Bliven, John, 131
Bradford, William, 76
Braddock, Edward, 51-52
Branch of a Tree, 152, 177
Brant, Joseph, 55, 79, 96-97, 122-124, 137, 148-153, 155, 179, 185
Brant, Molly, 45-46, 55, 147, 185
Brath, Henery, 153
Bronkahorse, 157
Brooke, Rupert, 41
Bull, Lt., 77
Bull, Mrs., 77
Burgoyne, John, xi, 3, 119-120, 184, 186
Burnett, William, 74
Butler, John, 96, 109, 122, 124, 148-149, 155, 162, 176, 180-182
Butler, Walter, 49, 96, 123, 183

Campbell, Maj., Douglas, 6
Campbell, Samuel, 6, 103, 130, 151
Campbell, William, 77
Carlton, Guy, 182
Caroline, 46
Casler, George, 151
Casler, Jacob, 150
deChamplain, Samuel, 29
Charles I, 121
Charles V, 67

Clapsaddle, Augustus, 131
Claus, Ann, 44-45
Claus, Daniel, 45, 80, 96, 100, 122-124, 148, 181, 185
Clinton, George, 48, 124-125, 181, 186
Clyde, Samuel, 79, 130, 157
Colbrath, William, 179, 181-182, 184
Conassatego, 31
Conkling, Roscoe, 4
Conyne, Peter, 131
Cornplanter, 148, 152
Cosby, William, 76
Cox, Ebenezer, 8, 102, 123, 130, 132-133, 145, 147, 150-151
Cox, Julian, 132
Cox, William, 158-159
Crouse, Robert, 101, 175
Custer, George, 3, 177

Davis, John James, 163-164
Dayton, Elisha, 102
DeLancey, James, 76, 78
Demuth, Han Marks, 132
Dering, Sylvester, 6, 11
DeRoville, Hertel, 149
Diefendorf, Henry, 158
Dieffendorf, Jacob, 151
Dieskau, Baron, 52, 54
Dillenbeck, Andrew, 162
Dinwiddie, Robert, 51
Doneraile, Viscount, 121
Doxtater, Han Yerry, 146, 160
Duesler, John, 155-156
Duquesne, Marquis, 51
Dygert, John, 177
Dygert, Maria, 103, 132, 178
Dygert, Peter, 180

Eaton, Adilda, 8
Eckler, Christopher, 155
Eisenlord, John, 97, 131
Everts, Chief of Staff, 7

Failing, Henry, 156, 163
Failing, Jacob, 159
Ferdinand of Hapsburg, 67
Fish Lapper, 152, 177
Flock, John, 157
Folts, Hon Yost, 132
Fonda, Adam, 102
Fonda, Henry, 79
Fonda, Jane, 79

Fonda, Jelles, 79
Fonda, Peter, 79
Fox, Charles, 120
Fox, Christopher W., 98, 157-159, 177
Fox, Peter, 158
Fralick, Valentine, 155
Franklin, Benjamin, 91, 105, 119
Franklin, William, 43
Fraser, McIntyre, 4
Frederick the Great, 97, 119
Frederick IV, 67
Frey, Hendrick, 96-97
Frey, John, 97, 130, 179

Gansevoort, x, Peter, 8, 13, 126-128, 132, 138, 147, 162, 179-180, 182-184
Gardenier, Jacob, 162-163
Garfield, James, 9
Gates, Horatio, 186
George I, 121
George II, 48
George III, 43, 78, 81, 93, 96-97, 104, 106-107, 123
Ginnis, Lt., 176
Gordon, Lord, 44
Graham, George, 5, 12
Grant, Ulysses, 4, 6
Graydon, Alexander, 106
Greeley, Horace, 4
Greene, Ann, 8
Greene, Emily, 8
Gregg, Capt. 127
Grenville, George, 93
Gros, Johan, 163

Hamilton, Andrew, 76
Hancock, John, 99
Hare, John, 155
Hayonwatha, 20-24, 35
Helmer, Adam, 132
Hendrick, 47, 50, 52-53, 71
Henry, Patrick, 94
Herkimer, Catherine, 74
Herkimer, George, 103
Herkimer, Johann Jost, Sr., 74, 79
Herkimer, Han Yost, Jr., 102, 130
Herkimer, Magdalena, 74
Herkimer, Nicholas, 8, 10-11, 65, 74, 78-79, 97, 101-103, 115, 122-125, 129-133, 137, 141, 145, 147, 150-152, 154, 159-161, 164, 173, 175, 178-179, 181, 183, 186
Herkimer, Warren, 8
Hess, John, 175
Hildebrand, Lt., 122, 148
Hood, John Bell, 10
Hooker, Joseph, 9
House, Christian, 159

Howe, William, xi, 105, 120
Hunt, Abel, 151
Hunter, Robert, 71-74
Hutchinson, Charles, 4
Hutchinson, Thomas, 94

Jackson, Stonewall, 9
James II, 96, 162
Jefferson, Thomas, 105
Jogues, Isaac, 31
Johnson, Brant, 46, 97
Johnson, Guy, 44-45, 79-80, 96, 100-104, 123
Johnson, John, 43-44, 96, 100-102, 122, 148-149, 152, 161-164, 176, 179, 181, 185-186
Johnson, Mary, 44, 79
Johnson, William, 41, 43-56, 75, 77, 79-81, 96, 104, 176
Johnson, William, of Canajoharie, 46, 148, 158
Johnston, Robert, 178, 183
Jones, Pomroy, 6

Kernan, Francis, 4
Kidd, William, 72
King, Alonzo, 6, 16
Kirkland, Samuel, 55, 79, 104, 123
Klock, George, 96-97
Klock, Jacob, 97-98, 102, 130, 132, 146, 150, 152-153, 159, 175
Klock, Johannes, 50
Knox, British Sec. of War, 185
Kocherthal, Joshua, 68-70

Lalemant, Gabriel, 31
Lansing, Mrs. Abraham, 8, 11, 13
Lee, Robert E., 6
deLery, Gaspard, 76-77
Leopold I, 67
Lewis, John, 178
Lincoln, Abraham, 5
Little Billy, 152
Livingston, Robert, 43, 72-73, 94, 105
Loucks, Adam, 97
Louis, 146, 160
Louis XIV, 67-68, 83, 97
Lovelace, Gov., 69
Lowery, Samuel, 4
Lyman, Phineas, 54-55
Lyons, Oren, 17
Luther, Martin, 67, 97

Macaulay, 68
Maddeson, Cpl., 127
Mansel, Lady, 121
Marlborough, 71
Marlett, John, 101
McDonald, Capt., 122, 163

McKinley, William, 4
Mellon, Lt. Col., 127
Merckley, William, 154
Miller, Adam, 155
Monckton, Robert, 51-52
Montgomery, Richard, 105
Morris, Robert, 43
Mowers, Conrad, 150

Newkirk, John, 131
Nickus, 55

Odatshedeh, 23
Old Smoke, 148, 152, 185

Paine, Thomas, 76
Paris, Isaac, 98, 130, 177
Parker, Arthur, 19
Parker, John, 99
Peacemaker, 19-20, 22-24, 34
Pearsee, Mary, 126
Pendergrast, William, 94
Penn, William, 69
Petri, Marcus, 77
Petrie, John, 161
Petry, William, 131, 178
Pickard, John, 130
Pierce, Franklin, 5
Pitcairn, John, 99
Porter, Joseph, 4-5
Potts, Dr., 183
Prince George of Denmark, 89
Proctor, Thomas, 7
Putnam, Clarissa, 44
Putnam, Richard, 164

Quackenbush, Adam, 156
Queen Anne, 45, 47, 69-71, 121, 185

Red Jacket, 35, 148, 152
Revere, Paul, 99
Roberts, Ellis, 4
Roof, Johannes, 78
Roosevelt, Theodore, 4

St. Germain, Count, 119
St. Leger, Barry, xi, 120-122, 124-125, 128-
    129, 136, 146-149, 175, 180, 183-184, 186
Sammons, Frederick, 100
Sammons, Jacob, 100, 151
Sammons, Sampson, 100
Sammons, Thomas, 100
Sanders, 55
Sanders, Henry, 159
Saxe, Marshall, 52
Schuyler, Han Yost, 183
Schuyler, Philip, 71
Schuyler, Peter, 71

Schuyler, Philip, 101-102, 112, 124, 175,
    183, 184
Scott, John, 126
Seeber, Audolph, 151, 156
Seeber, Jacob, 151, 156
Seeber, William, 130, 146, 151, 156
Seymour, Horatio, 3-4, 6, 8, 11-15
Seymour, John, 3, 13
Sherman, Roger, 105
Shirley, William, 48, 51-52
Shuckbaugh, Richard, 56
Shults, George, 156
Simms, Jeptha, 6
Singleton, Lt., 176
Snell, Jacob, 177
Spanable, John, 175
Spencer, Thomas, 146, 161
Sporr, Ensign, 127
Starin, John, 5, 9
Stanwix, John, 125
Stevens, James, 4
Stone, William, 123
Stuart, John, 79

Tahajadoris, 48
Things on the Stump, 151, 177
Thompson, Alexander, 186
Tice, Gilbert, 128
Townshend, Charles, 95
Trumbull, Gov., 104
Tryon, William, 81
Two Kettles Together, 160
Tygert, Warner, 101

VanAlstyne, Martin, 50
Van Deusen, Edward, 11-12
Van Eps, Jan, 159
Van Schaik, Goose, 127
Van Slyke, Harmanus, 97-98, 130, 151
Van Vechten, Anthony, 98, 130, 153
Veeder, John, 100
Veeder, Volkert, 131, 147, 153
Villars, Marshall, 68
Visscher, Frederick, 6, 97, 100, 102, 131-
    132, 146-147, 151-155, 163, 185
Visscher, Gazena, 146
Visscher, S.G., 6
von Steuben, Baron, 119

Wager, Daniel, 6, 15
Wagner, Alfred J., 5-8
Wagner, George, 156
Wagner, Johan Peter, 50
Wagner, Joseph, 123
Wagner, Peter, 5-6, 98, 102, 130, 146, 156
Wagner, Webster, 5-6
Wall, Edward, 101
Walter, George, 157

lrath, Garret, 158
lrath, Henry, 175
rren, Peter, 46
ashington, George, 51, 95, 105-106, 113,
9, 131, 182, 185
atts, Polly, 44, 100, 102
atts, Stephen, 122-163
Weed, Stephen, 10
Weissenberg, Catherine, 43, 45, 47
Weisser, Conrad, 73, 86
Wesson, Col., 127-128
Wheelock, Ebenezer, 55
White, Philo, 4-5, 16

Whiting, Col., 53
Willett, Marinus, 126-127, 138, 179-180,
182
William III, 162
Williams, Ephraim, 52-53
Williams, Othniel, 4
Wolfe, James, 121
Wormuth, 156

Yates, Christopher P., 98, 101
Younglove, Moses, 130, 159, 176, 178

Zenger, John Peter, 76

About the Author

Allan Foote is the President of the Mohawk Valley History Project company specializing in the research, development, and marketing of historical products such as books, films, music, board games, and computer software. *Liberty March* is the initial offering of this new company and Foote's first published work.

Foote has twenty years experience in management and marketing, primarily in the retail jewelry field. He currently serves as the Fine Jewelry Manager for the Harris Brothers Jewelers in New Hartford, New York. In the early 1980's, he served as a consultant/writer to the New York State Department of Education and was employed by the Division of Student Affairs, SUNY Albany, as a residence administrator and member of the faculty.

Mr. Foote has a B.A. in political science and a M.S. in higher education administration from the State University College at Buffalo. He has had a life-long interest in military history.

Foote has been involved with community organizations including, A Good Old Summertime Festival, Coliseum Soccer Club, the Board of Trustees of the Utica Public Library, and was the president of the Downtown Utica Development Association. In 1993, Foote was named as "Person of the Year" by the Utica Area Chamber of Commerce.

Foote has three teenage sons, Joshua, Jason, and Michael. He resides in Whitesboro, New York with his wife, Kathy, about four miles from the Oriskany Battlefield.

Allan D. Foote